Baghdad: An Urban History through the Lens of Literature

T0383575

In recent years, Baghdad has been viewed as a battleground for political conflicts; this interpretation has heavily influenced writings on the city. This book moves away from these perspectives to present an interdisciplinary exploration into the urban history of Baghdad through the lens of literature. It argues that urban literature is an effective complementary source to conventional historiography, using in-depth analysis of texts, poems and historical narratives of non-monumental urban spaces to reveal an underexamined facet of the city's development.

The book focuses on three key themes, spatial, nostalgic and reflective, to offer a new approach to the study of Baghdad's history, with a view to establishing and informing further strategies for future urban developments. Beginning with the first planned city in the eighth century, it looks at the urban transformations that influenced building trends and architectural styles until the nineteenth century.

It will appeal to academics and researchers in interdisciplinary fields such as architecture, urban history, Islamic studies and Arabic literature.

Iman Al-Attar is an Iraqi architect, historian and a doctor in philosophy and urban history. She was born in Baghdad, Iraq, and received her BA in Architecture from the University of Baghdad. She completed her MA in Urban Design at the University of Auckland before graduating with a PhD in Philosophy and Urban History from the University of Tasmania in 2014.

Al-Attar has participated in a number of conferences dealing with architectural history and heritage, and a number of her research papers have been published. She worked in urban planning for several years, and is currently doing research on topics including urban history, Islamic architecture, conservation and cultural issues.

Built Environment City Studies

The *Built Environment City Studies* series provides researchers and academics with a detailed look at individual cities through a specific lens. These concise books delve into a case study of an international city, focusing on a key built environment topic. Written by scholars from around the world, the collection provides a library of thorough studies into trends, developments and approaches that affect our cities.

Seville: Through the Urban Void
Miguel Torres

Amman: Gulf Capital, Identity and Contemporary Megaprojects
Majd Musa

Baltimore: Reinventing an Industrial Legacy City
Klaus Philipsen

Milan: Productions, Spatial Patterns and Urban Change
Edited by Simonetta Armondi and Stefano Di Vita

Baghdad: An Urban History through the Lens of Literature
Iman Al-Attar

Baghdad: An Urban History through the Lens of Literature

Iman Al-Attar

Routledge
Taylor & Francis Group

LONDON AND NEW YORK

First published 2019 by Routledge

2 Park Square, Milton Park, Abingdon, Oxfordshire OX14 4RN

52 Vanderbilt Avenue, New York, NY 10017

Routledge is an imprint of the Taylor & Francis Group, an informa business

First issued in paperback 2020

British Library Cataloguing-in-Publication Data
A catalogue record for this book is available from the British Library

Library of Congress Cataloging-in-Publication Data
Names: Al-Attar, Iman, author.
Title: Baghdad : an urban history through the lens of literature / Iman Al-Attar.
Other titles: Textual representations of the socio-urban history of Baghdad
Description: New York : Routledge, 2019. | Series: Built environment city studies | Originally presented as the author's thesis (doctoral—University of Tasmania, 2014) under the title: Textual representations of the socio-urban history of Baghdad : critical approaches to the historiography of Baghdad in the 18th and 19th centuries. | Includes bibliographical references and index.
Identifiers: LCCN 2018023212 | ISBN 9781138625440 (hardback) | ISBN 9780429459931 (ebook)
Subjects: LCSH: Urbanization—Iraq—Baghdad – History. | Baghdad (Iraq)—Historiography. | Baghdad (Iraq)—In literature.
Classification: LCC HT384.I6552 B333 2019 | DDC 307.7609567/47—dc23
LC record available at https://lccn.loc.gov/2018023212

ISBN: 978-1-138-62544-0 (hbk)
ISBN: 978-0-367-67044-3 (pbk)

Typeset in Times New Roman
by Apex CoVantage, LLC

To my daughters

Contents

Illustrations

Preface

This book presents long years of devotion to explore the architectural and urban history of Baghdad. Since the early years of my study in architecture, I have developed a passion and interest in discovering the 'real story' behind historical forms. I studied architecture at the University of Baghdad in the eighties of the twentieth century. Compared with new building styles, 'old' housing schemes, which belonged to the early decades of the twentieth century and the preceding period, were outlined as 'heritage'. At that time, there was a serious movement to protect 'heritage' and initiate planning guidelines to save what could be saved, and to implement original design patterns in new projects. Although conservation policies were relatively effective, they were mainly focused on the physical qualities of single buildings, with a little focus on social and nonphysical qualities. Subsequently, Baghdad's urban image continued to deform and lose its identity.

One of the projects in my second year of study was to document some unique historical houses in central Baghdad. These houses belonged to the late nineteenth century. While we took the measurements of every corner and drew concise architectural drawings, I felt the forms were mute and did not inform us much about the social circumstances and the inner meaning of this architecture. Every student admired the fascinating building styles and the unique ornamentations, in addition to the clever ideas that resolved weather and construction problems. Later, students started to embrace these styles into their design projects. Personally, I loved the idea of the courtyard and I started to incorporate it into my own projects. However, due to the lack of understanding of historical forms and the absence of strategies that utilise architectural history constructively, these attempts did not result in meaningful design schemes.

After graduating, and while I was working at the National Urban Planning Authority in Baghdad, these issues were challenged daily, but on a bigger scale that involved the design of the whole city. I started to write about heritage and conservation issues, and before I started my master's study in New Zealand, I participated in a conference that dealt with these issues. When I started my doctoral research in Australia in 2006, the topic of "textual representation of the socio-urban history of Baghdad" was suggested as the main focus of my thesis. As an architect whose way of thinking is related to science and geometry, I found it a complex and strange idea to represent the urban history of Baghdad by examining literature, which, as a discipline, has no direct connection to architecture or urban history. However, after a deep observation, I was fascinated by the method of literature interrogation, and the concept of opening architecture to other disciplines to enrich our understanding of architectural and urban history. This concept enabled me to find answers for many questions concerning the urban history of Baghdad.

This book verifies the effective role of literature as a 'complement' to other sources in Baghdad's historiography. It represents an attempt to discover more themes that would unveil the mysterious aspects of various urban experiences. The aim is to increase the understanding of the specific characteristics of Baghdad's urban history, and establish further strategies for future urban developments of Baghdad, based on this understanding. The book contains a few parts of my doctoral thesis; however, I have re-written everything and developed the contents to fulfil its objectives. Although this book focusses on the history of Baghdad in particular, I believe the method of investigation and the idea of interrogating literature can enrich urban history studies in general. The understanding of Baghdad's urban history before the twentieth century denotes more understanding of the urban history of other adjacent cities, such as Damascus and Istanbul, that shared similar circumstances with Baghdad. Besides, themes such as 'taste', 'smell', 'affection', 'friendship' and 'beauty' apply to other urban experiences all over the world, which adds to the significance of this study.

I would like to thank the staff of the University of Tasmania who contributed to the development and efficiency of this inquiry by providing books and resources. I would also like to extend my gratitude to my family and friends in Baghdad for their help in obtaining rare and old books. I obtained a precious old poetry book from my father's collection, which was invaluable to my research. Also thanks to my small family here in Australia for their support. Particular gratitude goes to my daughters Naba and Noor for their care and tolerance during the busy times of writing this book. In Australia, there is a significant body of architectural scholarship focusing on original eighteenth and nineteenth century Arabic sources emerging, and this book is a contribution to these studies. I hope this book enhances the efficiency and compatibility of future development plans that deeply consider the specific requirements of particular places, in Baghdad and everywhere.

Author's note

All translations from Arabic sources are mine, unless otherwise stated. The translations of poems are intended to convey the meaning of these poems rather than provide a literal translation. Where translations of the same text by others have been used, appropriate reference is given in the endnotes.

In transliteration, I have followed the system of *IJMES*. According to this system, diacritics are not added to personal names and place names. Diacritical scripts are used on technical terms, which are italicised and translated. Arabic terms known to English readers are italicised without translation.

All single dates are of the Common Era (CE) or Anno Domini (AD). Double dates are included to show additional *hijrī* dates (based on the Islamic calendar) in the following format: AH (*hijrī*)/AD. Alongside every name of an Arabic scholar there is the year when he died, in this format: (d. AH/AD).

Introduction

Baghdad is an ancient city with a unique urban history. It is the second largest city in the Arab world after Cairo. Due to the continuous political change in Baghdad, there is an increasing interest in its historical issues. This city has endured a fair share of damage over the centuries. However, the echo of its remarkable reputation in history still exists, which carries hopes of rebuilding it on a basis of solid and well-planned principles. Today, Baghdad is still experiencing constant destruction as a result of incessant wars. Yet, among the remarkable features of this city is its perseverance and its ability to survive various tribulations throughout history. The writings on Baghdad's urban history are few compared to other cities such as Cairo and Damascus. Even the available writings unevenly present different stages of the city's development. These issues motivate the researchers to delve deeper into this city's urban history.

The history of Baghdad encompasses enigmatic and mysterious aspects through its contradictory character of brilliance and gloominess in historical writings. Conventional historiography regards the availability of direct indications of urban developments in the literature of the early centuries of Baghdad's formation (mainly ninth and tenth centuries) as a sign of its prosperity. It also considers the decrease of such indications in the literature of the period after the fifteenth century as a sign of its decline. It is an inevitable fact that the history of cities is a connected chain of events that cannot be separated. Yet the lack of evidence of urban developments in literature does not necessarily imply a total absence of the city's advancement in reality. Rather, it indicates insufficient implementation of various techniques in the historical inquiry.

In historical studies, history has been questioned in terms of its capability to reveal the truth. The indefinite nature of history writing allows modification, depending on the purpose of writing; whether it be for political purposes, entertainment or just a documentation of events. In many cases, truth and fiction are neatly intertwined. This blurring can be dangerous if introduced as a technique in historiography.[1] The search for truth is a motivating tool that ignites historical inquiry and supplies it with energy and hope. However, absolute truth is not completely attainable, because of the distance between past and present, and the different interpretations of the notion of truth itself. So it is crucial to develop a critical scheme that allows our intellect to distinguish between these various ideas, to reveal the concealed features of Baghdad's history. Instead of achieving absolute truth, the search for truth in this book aims to reveal additional ideas in order to clarify truthful aspects of the past.

I introduced the method 'integrated interpretation' in this book as an aid to understanding the past. This method embraces a more integrated approach and fewer predetermined judgements. Integration simply implements multiple directions and avoids the preference of certain sources, thereby minimising bias statements. This approach assists in outlining interpretations that are not bound to narrow views or to single identifiers of objective and subjective methods, which confine research to one or two aspects of history. Integrative thinking is a step forward that touches on all aspects of humanity, and combines them with conceptual and spiritual qualities to improve understanding of the past. In addition to ideas, the method integrates different phases of history, to ensure its continuity. In this regard, time is viewed as an open space that continuously generates significance and meaning, and the integrative approach considers time as a dimension that intervenes deeply in human emotions.

It is important to note that new and conventional methods are not a dichotomy, as there is a constant negotiation in the use of both approaches in history writing. I believe implementing them mutually is a powerful tool that can aid the understanding of the history of cities. The difference between these techniques is that integrated interpretation initiates meaning and then moves to material qualities, while conventional interpretation start with material descriptions and attempts to formulate meaning afterwards. In other words, an understanding of history through the process of integrated interpretation relates to ideas rather than locations, and goes beyond the limitations of time and place.

Integrated interpretation in this book seeks another perspective in history, by considering literature as a source of valuable information that unveils the mysterious aspects of history and reveals more spatial concepts. It also promotes the interconnection of subjective and objective ideas, since texts convey a combination of both. The idea is to specify selected pieces of literature that were composed in the designated period for the study. These texts are interpreted according to the guidelines of the 'integrated interpretation' method to disclose truthful insights in relation to the urban characteristics of Baghdad at that time. In addition, the interpretation process implemented a thematic approach, to identify various concepts of urban history. The aim is to establish relationships between all perspectives of the past, and emphasise the interlocking factor in the communication between the historian and historical evidence.

Although this book examines the urban history of Baghdad in general, it provides a deep and detailed investigation of the eighteenth and nineteenth centuries in particular. The phase between the mid-eighteenth century and the mid-nineteenth century was a critical period of change, not just in Baghdad, but across the world. This period interconnects with the colonial era, and it is significant to the modern history of Baghdad, which makes it a momentous period of history. Along with other cities that were under Ottoman control, Baghdad experienced urban and political transformation. While still recognised as a great city, Baghdad lost its flourishing character in the eighteenth century due to recurrent conflicts and epidemics. However, in the early decades of the nineteenth century, Baghdad experienced architectural and urban developments that greatly improved its physical character. At the superficial level, by the mid-nineteenth century, it started to respond to stronger colonial influences.

In addition to the transformation and change that shaped Baghdad's urban history, this period produced rich poetry and narratives that comprised plentiful themes of the city's urban development. The term 'urban literature' is utilised to identify these texts, as a different way to read socio-urban history. Historians suggest that truthful claim of texts may have been the main reason for their marginalisation in modern historiography.[2] The investigation that was carried out in this book proved the capability of texts to uncover historical truths. These writings are seen as "windows through which glimpses of experiential aspects of architecture are seen".[3] However, the difficulty in dealing with the double meaning of metaphoric expressions in these texts complicates the interpretation process. The contradictory aspects of Baghdad's presentation in history appear widely in narratives, depending on the experience of the writer. This issue necessitates the inclusion of narratives from various periods in order to elaborate the urban history of Baghdad over time. This technique views time as a complete, coherent unit, and contributes to an integrated interpretation of history.

The focus of this book is on two kinds of literature; poetry and historical narratives. The writings by Baghdadi poets are shaped with sensitivity and affection, and reflected their inspirations of the past. As for historians, political relations were the material underpinning the knowledge of the past, as well as social affairs and personal interests. The various ideas expressed by those writers help to construct more realistic images of physical and social systems. They also increase the understanding of the urban history of Baghdad and fill the gaps of historical representation. These images can assist in developing stronger policies, since planning methods and conceptual frameworks need a deeper examination of both current and past circumstances.

The role of scholars as the best-educated group was crucial in the history of cities like Baghdad. They influenced the general condition of society, as well as cultural and educational conditions. Such scholars, who continued to live in Baghdad despite many hardships, contributed to the stability of society and the maintenance of belief in the community after each disaster that caused a great loss of life. The poetry of Kazim al-ʾUzari is very eloquent and unique, and it contains a great amount of self-expressions, and remarkable insights about urban and social characteristics of Baghdad. This makes it a great source of ideas about the urban history of Baghdad in that period. Also the historical narratives of ʿabd al-Rahman al-Suwaidi and the poetry of Salih al-Tamimi and others encompass distinctive expressions and notions. The exploration of the writings of these scholars instils in the reader the feeling they are diving into deep seas of knowledge, and discovering ideas that ultimately helped me personally to understand history. The analysis of these texts makes you face the challenges of understanding complex language terms, yet these challenges make it a pleasurable experience for the researcher.

In order to understand contextual matters of Baghdad, it is important to examine its foundation and its urban developments through history. The first chapter of this book highlights these issues, while the second chapter analyses the concept of textual representation and the method of integrated interpretation in more depth. The third chapter examines samples of texts composed after the foundation of the round city of Baghdad until the eighteenth century. This examination is part of the integrated interpretation approach that applies studying the urban history intermittently. Chapter Four analyses texts from the eighteenth and nineteenth centuries, to highlight unveiled depictions of the urban history of Baghdad at that time. This book is an attempt to add to current understanding of the urban history of Baghdad. Further studies are imperative, though, to reveal more factual aspects about this history.

Notes

1 Kellner, 'Time and narrative, by Paul Ricoeur: History and criticism, by Dominick LaCapra', pp. 1114–1120.
2 Morkoc, *A study of Ottoman narratives on architecture*, p. 307.
3 Morkoc, *A study of Ottoman narratives on architecture*, p. 139.

1 The urban history of Baghdad

The context of Baghdad

The case of Baghdad provides an excellent vehicle to investigate the general problem of historiography. The vague representation of Baghdad's urban spaces in historical studies and the shortage of architectural documentations, in addition to its long history of creative writings, make this case ideal for such kind of investigation. Baghdad is located on a strategic site that increased its significance as a commercial, social and political hub, and "made it at the same time a major inland port and a great centre of overland trade".[1] This unique location allowed a substantial mixture of different cultures. In addition, Baghdad has an outstanding history as an administrative centre and a hub of knowledge and learning for many centuries, along with its complex history of conquest. According to Ràuf, the case of Baghdad attracted historians because it was the hub of most human activities of a particular civilisation, which makes the history of the city a representative of human history in general.[2]

In a study that examines the foundation of Baghdad among three examples of symbolic appropriation of land, Grabar interrogates the original goals of establishing the round city, which was the first planned city in Baghdad's area. He questions an 'unknown component' of Baghdad's history, noting that many events contributed to the foundation of Baghdad, including political, economic, strategic, administrative and climatic influences. However, all these factors could apply to several other early settlements in Iraq, which raises questions about the specific features of Baghdad that differentiated it from others. He notes "it is therefore legitimate enough to suppose that something else was involved here".[3] Likewise, Warren points out the mysterious criteria of this city that "has never given its secrets lightly. Even among Muslim cities it has been reticent, its architectural splendours hidden behind high walls and within deep courtyards".[4] I presume these 'secrets' are the result of inconsistent representation of urban history, in addition to transmitting ideas without sufficiently analysing them.

The bright history of Baghdad is considerably outlined by historians, calling it "the city of peace, the capital of Islam, of noble rank and conspicuous virtue".[5] Further, they described it as "a city of no particular dimension, because it was a city of all dimensions, with life focusing on every aspect of human endeavour".[6] Cooperson recognises Baghdad's uniqueness among other cities; "only a traveller ignorant of the Arabic literary tradition could place Baghdad on equal footing with other towns on his itinerary".[7] These remarks highlight what is called the 'golden age' during the Abbasids period (168/785–232/847). Yet, examining the texts of this period shows that the amazement at the golden age is always related to the architectural forms and the political order, rather than social and environmental aspects.

A critical analysis of the written history of Baghdad during the golden age outlines an overemphasis on the characteristics of the round city of Baghdad that was founded in 144/762.[8] This history approves its astonishing composition that was palatial and not really an urban one, "to which none of the early Islamic cities corresponds".[9] The excitement for the round city was initiated by the Orientalists who have articulated the remarkable features of this city that represents 'the glories of medieval Islam'.[10] This glory became the focus of historical literature, particularly studies of Islamic art and architecture. The magnificent attributes of the city and the strong aesthetic and geometric criteria meet their anticipations about Islamic architecture as an 'expression of power',[11] a utopian experiment in a scientific order[12] and as a model of Islamic cities.[13] Since the round city has diminished completely, the major source for this city in historiography continues to be literary.

Apart from the round city myth, another cause of the vagueness of the urban history of Baghdad is that the name 'Baghdad' took multiple identities in historic writing. While some writings state the round city as Baghdad, other writings point to the second settlement of Baghdad, or the western or eastern part of the city, or the ancient settlement, or even the whole area of Baghdad that combines all settlements. Although the different settlements of Baghdad took different names in history, the name 'Baghdad' survived and remained as a representative of the identity of the place. The difficulty in distinguishing which definition of Baghdad is shown in specific writings creates a problem for Baghdad's historiography.

Another cause of the ambiguity of Baghdad's urban history is the shortage of original books. Available historical studies on Baghdad, specifically, are few compared with studies on other cities in the region, such as Cairo, Damascus and Istanbul. The continuous loss of original books due to constant floods, epidemics and conflicts made it extremely difficult to preserve these precious works. Nadia al-Baghdadi suggests the reason for the shortage of original books is that writers did not provide multiple copies.[14] Nevertheless, the existence of insufficient copies was not completely through individual choice; it also related to other social and political circumstances.

When conditions improved, presses were established in Baghdad's area, including the first printing press in *al-Kazimiyya* in 1821,[15] and *dār al-salām* press in Baghdad in 1833.[16]

On the other hand, Raymond notes an investigation into the historical sociology of Baghdad, showing that the reason behind the absence of the basic studies of Baghdad and the absence of documentation is due to the pre-eminence of French scholarship at that time, which lacked interest in 'British-controlled Iraq'.[17] European travellers who visited Baghdad in the eighteenth century were mostly German and French, while the travellers of the nineteenth century who visited Baghdad were mostly British and American.[18] Moreover, Bonine implies that the lack of awareness of the eighteenth century's texts of Baghdad is a result of political tension which may have curtailed the research and made it difficult to progress further.[19]

In fact, the case of Baghdad is complex if it was portrayed from political perspectives. Yet, one of the most distinctive aspects of Baghdad is its attractiveness and prestige. This city has been a major source of inspiration for poets throughout its history to a degree that almost all scholars mentioned it and its river (Tigris River) in their writings. The following is an example of a recent poetic work by shaykh Aḥmad al-Waʾili:

> Oh Baghdad, your face will remain glorious and attractive
> No matter if the atmosphere was terrible or superior
> Every time I examine your originality closely
> My admiration for you increases more
> Different races added different bloods to your character
> Yet they didn't change your distinguished origins
> Many intellectual tributaries flowed in your river
> They seduce the minds and astonish the brains[20]

In this poem, al-Waʾili questions the reasons for Baghdad's attractiveness, and implies that eternal beauty of the city prompted its love. He associates the flow of the Tigris River with scholarly motivation, which highlights this river and educational events among the compelling aspects of Baghdad. This designates the unknown secret of attachment to Baghdad that started to grow gradually, as "nearly every generation of writers has felt the same way, with as much or as little justification".[21]

The urban history of Baghdad

The beginnings of Baghdad's history is controversial. While some historians claim it starts in the eighth century with the foundation of the round city, others verify that Baghdad's history goes back to four thousand years ago. Among the evidences of its old age is that it was mentioned in documents of King Hammurabi in 1750 BC. Also, the Aramaic word *bakdādu* was engraved on the old Babylonian mud stone that was discovered in 1780.[22] Moreover, the close proximity of Baghdad to the historical cities of Babylon, *dūr kūrigalzu, 'Ur* and *Nineveh*, from which ancient civilisations emerged, confirms its ancient history. Although most of the existing urban forms were inherited from the period following Islam,[23] the cityscape of Baghdad and the traces of architectural and urban forms reflect the diversity that resulted from this long urban history.

Historians bring up different interpretations of the word 'Baghdad'. For example, Cooperson links it to a Persian interpretation, as *bāgh* means 'idol' and *dād* means 'gift'.[24] The overall meaning of those different names, in general, indicates a fertile city, blessed with greenery and considered a gift from God.[25] This city has an intimate relationship with the Tigris River, which provides beauty, fertility and utility. This river runs through Baghdad, creating a beautiful environment and granting the surrounding area with a blissful and enduring reality. Together with the central location of Baghdad, the fertile land turned the ancient settlement in the area into a great market village. This village that was known as 'suq Baghdad' existed before Islam on the east side of the Tigris River.[26] The name of this village suggests the existence of the marketplace as a predominant activity of the city.

The flourishing phase of 'suq Baghdad' temporarily came to an end in the year 144/762, when a nearby site was chosen by the Abbasids' ruler, al-Mansur, to be the capital of the Abbasid's state.[27] A round city was constructed there, and this new settlement carried a number of names, including *al-zawra', madīnat* al-Mansur and *dār al-salām* (the house of peace), though it also maintained the original name, Baghdad. Later on, it attained additional names in the historical material such as the round city and the circular city. The round city settlement was built in *al-karkh* on the west side of the Tigris River, in an area called now (*al-'utayfiyya*).[28] The site was selected at a point where the two great rivers, Tigris and Euphrates, are closest to each other.

The round city basically constituted a circular centripetal geometric form, which is 2300 metres in diameter,[29] with double walls that had four double gates and a huge palace in the centre, in addition to the central mosque. It also comprised four market complexes in the arcades by each gate. Various neighbourhoods were located between the gates, and the caliph's palace was built in the centre of the city near the central mosque. This city was built of a relatively high standard. Historians are overwhelmed by the water supply system, which constituted efficient canals that pass through the quarters and among the dwellings.[30] The round city was heavily decorated and it contained many palaces, with neat and wide roads. It was planned in order to provide a high level of security to the caliph, by constructing numerous walls and gates[31] (Figure 1.1).

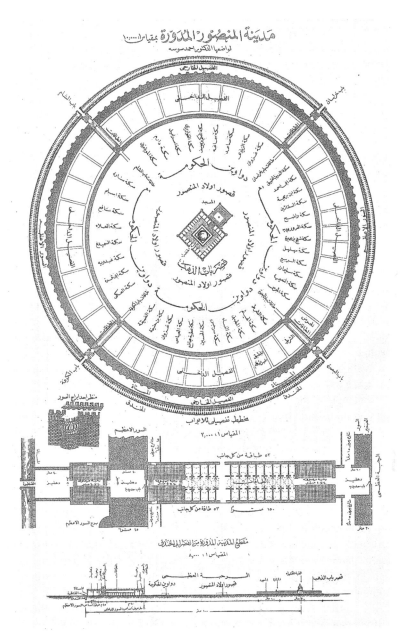

Figure 1.1 The plan of the round city of Baghdad

Source: Susa (1952).

After five years of building, the construction of the round city concluded in 149/767, and diverse groups of people immigrated to Baghdad to reside there. Muhammad 'Ali notes many people chose to reside in the round city, including merchants, different scholars, artists, craftsmen and all people who sought fame.[32] As a result, Baghdad became an international city associated with different people from many nationalities and backgrounds. However, shortly after its completion, the suburbs started to extend outside, as new buildings were constructed around the walled area closer to the river, shifting over one kilometre southwards from the city's original position, establishing a growing urban settlement (*al-karkh*) to the western bank of the Tigris.[33] This settlement reached out to the eastern bank of the Tigris,[34] generating the district of *al-rusafa*. The two parts, *al-karkh* and *al-rusafa*, constituted the city's main fixed components. With the river in the middle, they resemble two pages in a book.

Lassner notes the round city was "the first city expanded so rapidly and transformed itself so completely a few years after its creation".[35] In addition to the expansion outside the round walls that changed the demographic status of the round city, its affluence did not last longer than sixty-nine years, when the Abbasids moved their capital, from north Baghdad to Samarra' in 221/836.[36] Historical material indicates both the physical surface of the round city and its institutions were undergoing enormous changes after the decline. Subsequently, the city vanished completely,[37] and despite great excavation efforts, the Department of Antiquities in Baghdad could not find any trace of it.[38]

Nonetheless, the glory of the round city remained the focus of historical literature, and "the memory of its original shape and the ideas behind it lasted for centuries in a way that has no parallel in the history of Islamic cities".[39] An enormous amount of literature places it as the foremost great urban centre[40] and "the best city on earth".[41] Grabar links the reason for the city's exceptional standing in historiography to its shape that "was transformed through its internal composition into a symbolic and ceremonial palace, while maintaining a sort of token urban element in carefully measured, mapped out, and selectively settled quarters between the forbidding fortified walls and the abode of the caliph".[42] He suggests this city illustrates early Islamic monumental activities, and demonstrates the symbolic as well as physical appropriation of land in a particularly unusual style, even though nothing remains of it.[43]

It is correct that the round city was the first planned city in the history of Baghdad, and it has been unceasingly admired by the city dwellers. Yet relating the beginning of the history of Baghdad to the round city foundation, and the exaggeration of its status, are among the major tricks in Baghdad's historiography, since the history of dwellings in Baghdad goes a long way before that period. As outlined previously, the life span of the round city was short, and it started to deteriorate gradually until it disappeared. However, the memory of its original shape and the ideas behind it lasted for centuries in a way that has no equivalent in the history of other cities in the region. This city has also been admired by Baghdadi dwellers, who expressed an imaginative appreciation of it in their writings. The remembrance of the round city was a stimulus to be positive about the future, since it keeps reminding them of a great history.

The rapid decline of the round city is due to several possible reasons. The firm round shape that resisted expansion stimulated the expansion outside its walls. Also, the round city was built away from the river for security reasons. Historically, the Tigris River has been a major part of the urban appeal of Baghdad, so the relative remoteness from the waterway encouraged the expansion outside the city, and contributed to the city's weakening. Moreover, political decisions like building double layers of fences around military bases, and establishing prisons in the basements, increased social disaffection to the city. After it was deserted, continuous floods contributed to its destruction.

It appears that, in addition to being far from the river, expelling craftsmen and merchants outside the city was among the main causes of hastening the decline of this city, as shifting the market activity closer to the river encouraged growth outside it. At the beginning, the markets were constructed inside the round city, but they were moved shortly afterwards. Al-'Alusi narrates a story that explains the reason behind the markets' expulsion. He quotes from al-Khatib al-Baghdadi that one day a delegate from the Byzantine Empire visited the caliph al-Mansur and expressed his astonishment about the round city. He then stated that the round city would be perfect except for three shortcomings. First, the city was far away from the river. Second, there was not much greenery, and third, the markets were inside the city,[44] warning the caliph about foreigners and enemies who may penetrate through the markets at any time, as no one can be denied access to those markets.[45] The caliph ordered the markets to be moved, to ensure his own security and to keep the noise outside the city. Moving the markets decreased the liveliness of the city and evoked opposite movement. Consequently, the old settlement of suq Baghdad that was developed late into the district of *al-rusafa* regained its significance. The unique map that was produced by ibn Hawqal in 367/978[46] shows Baghdad in the middle of the country, with the two parts *al-karkh* and *al-rusafa* that were almost equal in size (Figure 1.2). This reflects the continuous growth of *al-rusafa* two hundred years after the construction of the round city.

In the year 278/892 the Abbasids moved their capital from Samarra' back to Baghdad.[47] Instead of returning to the round city, it was *al-rusafa* they

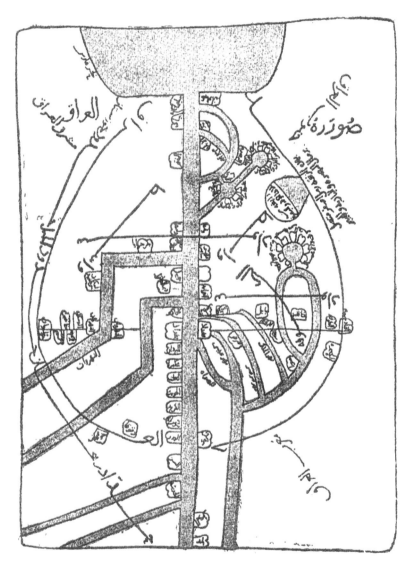

Figure 1.2 A map of Iraq by ibn Hawqal in the tenth century
Source: Jawad and Susa (1958).

selected for their new residence, "abandoning the previous northern settlements and confirming the shift of the urban system which had occurred".[48] The second settlement of the Abbasids in *al-rusafa* comprised the centre of Baghdad's important divisions, and the markets kept attracting inhabitants, and later businesses, and became the commercial core of Baghdad for centuries to the present day. The proximity of *al-rusafa* to the eastern trade routes, its location on slightly higher land and the extensive existence of markets associated with revered tombs and mosques[49] may explain its prolonged existence.

The Abbasids erected more palaces and bridges, which gained a great deal of attention in literature because of their outstanding features. The lavish and luxurious life that the young caliphs experienced in Baghdad drew their attention away from administration and turned their rule to a 'local monarchy'.[50] The second settlement of the Abbasids in *al-rusafa* lasted for a long time and continued to be the central hub for successive governments, including Ottomans. This settlement added to the existing settlement, was not restricted to a geometrical shape (Figure 1.3), and was not founded on unjust political and peculiar desires. Many buildings survived from this settlement, and they can inform the historical query. However, the second settlement did not receive a similar interest to that of the round city in the conventional historiography, which indicates the need to carefully examine Baghdad's urban history in order to discover these circumstances.

It is important to note that the Baghdad that is described in literature is not always the same type of settlement of Baghdad, yet the popular vision of the round city limits the perspective of Baghdad to it. The Abbasids ruled Baghdad for four hundred and thirty-five years. The span of their rule in the round city did not exceed sixty-nine years, which leaves a longer period of three hundred and sixty-six years to the second settlement of Baghdad. In fact, reading the literature by local scholars reveals it is the second settlement of Baghdad that comprised elegant mansions and thriving markets. In this period, Baghdad became a great centre of theological study, as well as more general learning, which for centuries attracted many people to live there. After the Abbasids period, the adoration of local poets was to their current Baghdad, despite its relatively negative visual appeal, especially towards the eighteenth century. Still, literature shows various expressions of pride, admiration, sympathy, ingratitude and dislike.

The monumental and emblematic presentation made Baghdad "the navel of the universe, and medieval geographers put Iraq in the central and most favoured clime of the world".[51] Cooperson suggests the glories of the Abbasids' Baghdad and the colossal criteria associated with its attributes had instilled a lively appreciation among British observers,[52] who view it as an elaborate establishment rather than a simple settlement. The admiration of

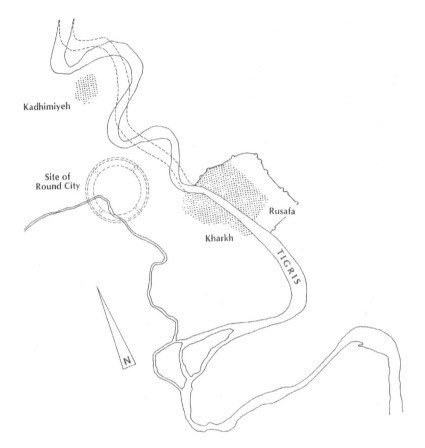

Figure 1.3 The round city on the western side of the Tigris and the second settlement on the eastern side

Source: Warren and Fethi (1982).

the Abbasids' Baghdad is also expressed in the literature of Baghdadis, but
from a different perspective. For example, al-'Alusi explains this common
historical vision, noting that Baghdad was a great Abbasid's city that was
laughing until Hulago Khan made it cry with blood.[53] The dismal circumstances that accompanied the long history of Baghdad, and the extensive
narratives that exaggerate its standards and illustrate a city free of the troubles, turned the round city and Abbasid's Baghdad into a nostalgic icon that
evokes admiration and longing.

This case can be considered one of the most contradictory cases in Baghdad's urban history. While some texts emphasise the measures of a thriving city that arouse romantic expressions and increase the will to settle there, sometimes the second settlement is mentioned as a subsidiary to the round city. Although combining the two settlements in literature connected the physical characteristics of the round city with the astonishing architecture and high educational facilities of the second settlement, it causes a difficulty in historiography to designate which Baghdad is meant by specific texts. Yet undoubtedly the second settlement that grew on the shores of the Tigris River, without any planned geometrical form or restriction of movement, gained more affection, which was clearly reflected in texts.

In 334/946 Persian Buyids controlled the western side of Baghdad, in addition to a few areas in the eastern part. This invasion might have been a reflection of the weakness of late Abbasids' caliphs due to their immersion in a luxurious lifestyle. In 443/1052 Turkish Seljuk took over parts of Baghdad.[54] It can be assumed that the beginning of the political tension in Baghdad between these two growing powers in the area (Persians and Turkish) started in this time period. The Abbasids took Baghdad back in 582/1187, but in 683/1258 the Mongols invaded it and put a distinct end to the Abbasids' rule. At this point, the historiography of Baghdad started to take a dramatic turn. Historians mark this year as the year of the 'fall of Baghdad', which draws a sharp end to the earlier prosperous and flourishing life of the city.

Apparently, literature exaggerates the terrible situation of the city after the Mongols' invasion, in contrast to the extremely positive mode before this date. There is no doubt the Mongols' invasion caused a lot of damage to the city, but in reality, the life of ordinary people did not change as drastically as some historians make it out to be and continued to fluctuate in the following centuries. An example of this contradiction is the description of an old painting of Baghdad, which portrays the devastating effects of a flood that took place in Baghdad in 757/1356 (Figure 1.4). While some writings link this image to a flood of the fourteenth century,[55] others link it to the Mongol invasion.[56] According to Mustafa Jawad and Ahmed Susa, the poem that is written on the upper part of this image that was written by al-Zakani did not mention the year,[57] yet another poet, Salman al-Sawji, who was a contemporary of al-Zakani, wrote a poem in Persian language stating that this flood had taken place in 757/1356.[58] This implies there is no link between this image and the Mongol invasion to Baghdad that took place about a hundred years earlier. The date ascribed to it in the British Museum collection is 1468[59] instead of 1356, which confirms the

Figure 1.4 A painting miniature of Baghdad

Source: British Library.

capability of history to alter confused facts easily. The following is a translation of that poem:

In the year 757AH rain devastated the great city drastically
Houses were damaged and the soil mixed with water
Oh Baghdad, the paradise of the world, I feel sorry for you
Your houses were destroyed by nature[60]

Some texts illustrate a more realistic image of both destruction and repara-
tion of physical structures. For example, Cooperson states that ibn Battuta
"found much to admire there even after the first Mongol onslaught".[61] Also,
Fletcher states in the century that followed the Mongol invasion, there was
something of an 'architectural revival' after the fall of Baghdad.[62] Likewise, scholars like al-Qazwini and al-Qasi al-Baghdadi, who lived after this
period, illustrate Baghdad as an object of wish and desire, an unsurpassed
centre comparable to paradise, and "the mother of the world, the mistress
of nations".[63] These remarks prove a continuous role of Baghdad – in the
fourteenth century – as an administrative centre and a venue of knowledge
and learning.

After the Mongols' invasion, Baghdad became a target for a crowd of
empires. In 802/1400 a group called Jalayirids controlled Baghdad, and
in 813/1411 it became occupied by Turkmens. In less than one hundred
years the Safavids controlled it in 913/1508, and in 940/1534, the Ottomans seized power over Baghdad. Then the Safavids took over it again
in 1030/1621 until 1047/1638 when the Ottomans regained control. The
Mamluks started to govern Baghdad from the beginning of the eighteenth
century, yet the year 1136/1750 marked the beginning of the autonomous
rule of the Mamluks, which continued to 1246/1831 when the Ottomans
controlled it completely, until the British occupation in 1335/1917.[64] Historians call the age that starts with the Mongols' occupation in 683/1258 and
ends with the British occupation in 1335/1917 the 'intermediary history'
that lasted for eight centuries. The period following 1917 until now is considered the 'modern history' of Baghdad.

This brief illustration of the political history of Baghdad shows the transitory conditions and temporality of Baghdad's historical accounts, which
reflected significantly on its material structures. It is true that the age of
empires, or what Crinson calls 'abstractions',[65] brought an entire era of
instability. With their intertwining effects on the city and their intermittent phases, those colonial forces left tangible imprints on culture and on
the society, and strongly influenced the city's morphology. However, the
rich heritage of creative writings on different branches of knowledge, and
the unique architectural styles that were developed towards the end of this

period, assert that it is unreasonable to label the 'intermediary history' as a part of 'dark ages'. Also, the analysis of urban literature in this book confirms the urban developments in this period.

Historical accounts of Ottoman cities

As outlined in the previous section, Baghdad was under the Ottomans' control from the sixteenth century up to the early twentieth century. In the period between the mid-eighteenth century and the mid-nineteenth century, it was controlled by the Mamluks, who were officially allied to the Ottomans. Thus, it is important to elaborate on Ottoman historical accounts and outline some characteristics of Ottoman cities. Ottoman history is a growing subject in current historical studies. These studies provide specific links to the critical moments of transformation and change in various standards of the cities that were under the Ottoman control. Most studies of Ottoman cities in the eighteenth century are centred on questions of aesthetics and affluence, such as public order, arts and entertainment. Hence, they can be considered as contributions to institutional history rather than proper urbanism.[66]

Nonetheless, a significant shift in attitudes towards general urban affairs is evident in some studies. For instance, Veinstein explores the possibility of the survival of a unique type of town characteristic of the Ottoman Empire that could naturally be stamped as 'Ottoman Town'. He notes that Istanbul sultans were interested in the city, and they developed a proactive urban policy that was implemented in various ways and at different levels.[67] He proposes there was a policy of differentiation between different cities controlled by the Ottomans, since Ottoman towns experienced specific conditions connected to their integration into the empire. Those conditions benefited specific towns unevenly, depending on the positions of these towns in the political, administrative, strategic and economic system of the empire.

Veinstein suggests Istanbul was privileged being both the main centre of attraction for all the empire's commercial exchanges and the primary object of imperial concern in terms of settlement, supplies, facilities, developments and beautification. He determines location as a measure for differentiation between Ottoman cities based on the greater or lesser distance from the capital. In addition, he proposes another reason for this disparity, which is a 'dividing line' that places Arabic provinces on one side and Anatolia and non-Arabic areas on the other. He notes this explains why historic Middle Eastern cities rank far behind Istanbul in the classification of the empire's main cities.[68] Besides having been considered fundamentally different, Arabic and central provinces "have been studied rather differently by different people".[69]

It is reasonable that distance might be a distinguishing element due to the difficult transportation circumstances at that time. It is also acceptable that the Ottoman sultans gave considerable attention to the architectural development in their capital Istanbul more than other cities. However, despite being Arabic, cities like Aleppo and Damascus were among the Ottoman territories that were "strikingly urbanised, when compared with Europe".[70] These cities could have maintained a great level of prosperity, but they lost relative importance during the eighteenth century with the drying up of the Iranian silk trade.[71] Therefore, apart from language or distance, it seems that there have been other factors in the decline of these cities, such as economic situations.

Despite being fundamentally different, Veinstein notes that the integration of different cities into the immense Ottoman structure was a sign of prosperity, and that this integration brought relative order, security and unified legislations. In terms of art and architecture, he suggests those measures contributed to a certain standardisation of production, although different situations provoked obvious divergences in architectural styles and terminology. The signs of order in Ottoman cities were related to the Islamic system. Undoubtedly the cities under the Ottomans' control shared similar features occasionally. The similarities were the consequences of the parallel laws enforced on those areas and easy movement between different regions in the empire. Still, the divergence was mainly a result of different political circumstances.

In the 1830s, the municipal reforms that came in the context of Tanzimat (reform laws) began in the Ottoman Empire. These reforms were characterised by various attempts to 'modernise' the Ottoman Empire. According to Veinstein, the unified measures drawn by the Tanzimat were "stimulated by developing relations with the West".[72] Lafi indicates that Europe in the mid-nineteenth century was not an island of modernity, and French historiography "has also insisted on the importation tool".[73] She states "there was in every Ottoman city an old regime urban system",[74] thus the reform laws were not importations into a blank canvas, and they were only partially influenced by Europeans. Undoubtedly, the unique urban system was associated with Ottoman cities before the nineteenth-century reforms. This system would certainly be a point of pride for the inhabitants, and what Lafi calls as the 'notability' who carried the urban government in their hands.[75]

In regards to Baghdad, it is important to note that the Baghdad area during the Ottoman period was larger than the city at present. Iraqi land was incorporated into three main provinces: Baghdad, Basra and Mosul[76] (Figure 1.5). Baghdad consisted of a number of cities that currently have separate municipalities. In the eighteenth century, Baghdad experienced damage to architectural structure. With 'little building activity',[77] the city became less

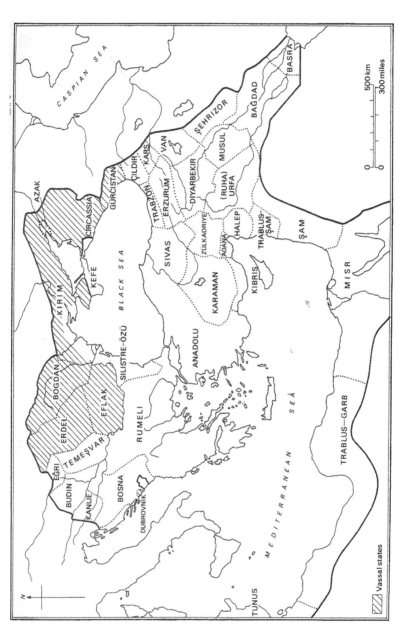

Figure 1.5 The Ottoman Empire and the provinces of Iraq

Source: Inalcik and Quataret (1997).

appealing, compared with other cities. The reason for this change was due to continuous fights between different groups, in addition to floods and epidemics. These bases overrule geographical proximity and ethnic diversity. Furthermore, the empire's provinces of Mosul, Baghdad and Basra "were often regarded as significant only in a military sense".[78] So, architectural and urban development in Baghdad and other Iraqi cities did not possess a priority in the government plans, since they were the frontier lines of the empire.

Notes

1 Lassner, *The topography of Baghdad in the early middle ages*, p. 17.
2 Rāuf, *maʿālim Baghdad fī al-qurūn al-mutākhira*, p. 3.
3 Grabar, *The formation of Islamic art*, p. 68.
4 Warren & Fethi, *Traditional houses in Baghdad*, p. 18.
5 Cooperson, 'Baghdad in rhetoric and narrative', pp. 99–113.
6 Lassner, *The topography of Baghdad in the early middle ages*, p. 17.
7 Cooperson, 'Baghdad in rhetoric and narrative', pp. 99–113.
8 The details of the foundation of the round city of Baghdad are discussed later in this chapter.
9 Grabar, *The formation of Islamic art*, p. 70.
10 Lewis, *History: Remembered, recovered, invented*, p. 97.
11 See Mitchell, *Colonising Egypt*. Also see Grabar, *The formation of Islamic art*.
12 Moholy-Nagy, *Matrix of man*, p. 60.
13 Moholy-Nagy, *Matrix of man*, p. 81. Also see Grabar's remarks about the plan of Baghdad in Aga Khan Award for Architecture, p. 35.
14 Al-Baghdadi, 'From heaven to dust: Metamorphosis of the book in pre-modern Arab culture', pp. 83–107.
15 Selman, 'al-Kazimiyya fī aʿmāq al-tārīkh'.
16 Al-Haydari, 'ṣafaḥāt min tārīkh al-kutub wal-kutubiyyin fī suq al-Sarāy'.
17 Raymond, 'Urban life and Middle Eastern cities: The traditional Arab city', p. 207.
18 Examples of the eighteenth century travellers: Carsten Niebuhr, Olivier and Mirza ʾabu Talib Khan. Examples of the nineteenth century travellers: Buckingham and Fogg.
19 Bonine, 'Islamic urbanism, urbanites and the Middle Eastern city', p. 403.
20 Al-Wāili, *diwān al-Wāili*, p. 68. The Arabic script:

سيظلّ وجهك رائعا جذّابا	بغداد ساء بك الهوى أم طابا
أمعنت فيها زدتني أعجابا	بغداد أيّ أصالة بك كلّما
لكنها ما غيّرت أحسابا	صبَت بك الأعراق مختلف الدما
تغوي النّهى وتحيّر الألبابا	وجرت بنهرك للعقول روافد

21 Cooperson, 'Baghdad in rhetoric and narrative', p. 103.
22 Al-Warid, *ḥawādith Baghdad fī 12 qarn*, p. 228.
23 Islam arose in the year 611.
24 Cooperson, 'Baghdad in rhetoric and narrative', pp. 99–113.
25 Jawad, Susa, Makkiya, & Maʿruf, *Baghdad*, p. 16.
26 Rāuf (ed.), *al-ʿiqd al-lāmiʿ bi-ʾāthār Baghdad wal-masājid wal-jawāmiʿ*, p. 20. See also Muhammad Ali, *madīnat Baghdad*.

22   The urban history of Baghdad

27 The Abbasids state lasted between 750 and 1258.
28 Ráuf, *tārīkh hawādith Baghdad wal-Basrah*.
29 Grabar, *The formation of Islamic art*, p. 68.
30 Lassner, *The topography of Baghdad in the early middle ages*, p. 100. Also see Ráuf, *'akhbār Baghdad wa mā jāwarahā min al-bilād*, p. 58.
31 See Susa, *Atlas Baghdad*.
32 Muhammad Ali, *Madinat Baghdad*, p. 161.
33 Lassner, *The topography of Baghdad in the early middle ages*, p. 27.
34 The settlement in the eastern part existed thousands of years before *al-karkh* settlement, yet it was expanded during that period.
35 Lassner, *The topography of Baghdad in the early middle ages*, p. 15.
36 The age of the city is counted from the year 767 when the construction concluded, until 836 when they moved to Samarrá.
37 Cooperson, 'Baghdad in rhetoric and narrative', pp. 99–113.
38 See Ráuf, *ma'ālim Baghdad fī al-qurūn al-mutākhira*. Also see Lassner, *The topography of Baghdad in the early middle ages*.
39 Grabar, *The formation of Islamic art*, p. 67. Some historical scholarship associates the round shape to pre-Islamic city design. See Moholy-Nagy, *Matrix of man*, pp. 55–61.
40 Lassner, *The topography of Baghdad in the early middle ages*, p. 25.
41 Cooperson, 'Baghdad in rhetoric and narrative', pp. 99–113.
42 Grabar, *The formation of Islamic art*, p. 71.
43 Grabar, *The formation of Islamic art*, p. 69.
44 Ráuf (ed.), *'akhbār Baghdad wa mā jāwarahā min al-bilād*, p. 58.
45 Lassner, *The topography of Baghdad in the early middle ages*, p. 61.
46 Jawad & Susa, *Dalil kharitat Baghdad al-Mufassal*.
47 See Ráuf (ed.), *'akhbār Baghdad wa mā jāwarahā min al-bilād*, p. 58. Also see Selman, *al-'imarat al-'arabiyya al-Islamiyya fī al-Iraq*.
48 Bianca, *Urban form in the Arab world*, p. 249.
49 The western side also contains a sacred site for sh'ia Muslims, northern *al-Karkh*, called al-Kazimiyya, after the burial of Imam Musa al-Kazim in 183/799.
50 Fletcher, *Sir Banister Fletcher's a history of architecture*, p. 532.
51 Grabar, *The formation of Islamic art*, p. 71.
52 Cooperson, 'Baghdad in rhetoric and narrative', pp. 99–113.
53 Ráuf (ed.), *'akhbaar Baghdad wa mā jāwarahā min al-bilād*, p. 44. Al-'Alusy refers to the Mongol invasion of Baghdad in 1258, which ended the Abbasid's rule.
54 For more details see Al-Warid, *hawādith Baghdad fī 12 qarn*.
55 Makkiyya (ed.), *Baghdad*, p. 76. Also see Jawad, Susa, Makkiyya, & Ma'ruf, *Baghdad*, p. 36.
56 Warren & Fethi, *Traditional houses in Baghdad*, p. 8.
57 The poem on the upper part of the painting states:

> *Dijla* this year had a behaviour that seemed very drunk-like
> Its feet is in chains and has its hand on its lips as if it was mad
> Water would run around and return as if it has set a siege
> Baghdad as if it had become a candle and *dijla* like a butterfly around it

58 Makkiyya (ed.), *Baghdad*, p. 76.
59 British Library Mss. Add. 16561, folio 60, recto, dated 1468.

60 Makkiyya (ed.), *Baghdad*, p. 76. Original Persian poem:

بسال هفصد بنجاه و هفت خراب   بآب شهر معظم كه خاك سراب
دریغ روضة بغداد ان بهشت اباد   كه كرده است خرابش سبهلا خانه خراب

61 Cooperson, 'Baghdad in rhetoric and narrative', pp. 99–113.
62 Fletcher & Musgrove, *Sir Banister Fletcher's a history of architecture*, p. 605.
63 Cooperson, 'Baghdad in rhetoric and narrative', p. 101.
64 Khayyat, *'arba'at qurūn min tārīkh al-Iraq al-ḥadīth*.
65 Crinson, *Modern architecture and the end of empire*, p. 4.
66 An example of these studies: Atasoy, 'Ottoman garden pavilions and tents', pp. 15–19.
67 Veinstein, 'The Ottoman town', pp. 207–212.
68 Veinstein, 'The Ottoman town', pp. 207–212.
69 Veinstein, 'The Ottoman town', pp. 207–212.
70 Inalcik & Quataert, *An economic and social history of the Ottoman Empire*, p. 646. For more about the Ottoman town, see Cerasi, 'The urban and architectural evolution of the Istanbul divanyolu', pp. 189–232.
71 Inalcik & Quataert, *An economic and social history of the Ottoman Empire*, p. 673.
72 Veinstein, 'The Ottoman town', pp. 207–212.
73 Lafi, 'The Ottoman municipal reforms between old regime and modernity', p. 355.
74 Lafi, 'The Ottoman municipal reforms between old regime and modernity', p. 354.
75 Lafi, 'The Ottoman municipal reforms between old regime and modernity', p. 356.
76 Tripp, *A history of Iraq*.
77 Ghaidan, 'Damage to Iraqi's wider heritage', p. 85.
78 'Abdullah, *Merchants, Mamluks and murder*, p. 6.

2 Textual representation of architecture

Texts and historical understanding

The idea of reading architecture from text is among the 'tools' suggested by architectural historians to promote the understanding of architecture. Because people are still collectively envisioning it through its physical body, architecture is often recognised by pictorial images. Morkoc notes "interpreting the architectural images from historical texts is useful for highlighting the multivalent historical experience of architecture".[1] The analysis of texts is necessary to obtain abstract reflections of place by differentiating the chronological layers of the text. Since "texts and architecture have commonality in expressing cultural values and therefore in embodying meaning, [t]hey are both products of mental mechanisms standing in between experience and reality".[2] The important aspect of studying urban history from text is that this process offers a deeper understanding of the city, its foundation and its connections at many levels, including constitutional, political, environmental and social.

Although textual metaphor has been used in architecture, reading architecture as a text has not been considered as an effective source in historiography, because of the extensive focus of postmodern thought on the objective criteria of urban history. Besides this, the issue of interpreting texts to extract architectural meaning has been questioned for its validity in providing access to the layers of meanings of the historical experience and reliability as a source for architectural understanding. However, textual representation of architecture is gradually becoming a major source of architectural historiography, because it has the potential to unveil unknown historical material and promote more understanding of the architectural and urban experiences. It is important to note that textual representation is not implemented in this book because of the shortage of sufficient images and historical material of Baghdad's history. The purpose of interrogating literature is to expand current methods to increase historical understanding, regardless of the place and timing of the historical event.

The prevailing method of architectural historical studies in relation to Baghdad and the Islamic world usually examines historical texts by visualising architecture as a mass, and searching for the interpretation of architecture through exploring the ideas represented in historical texts. In the last several decades, this scheme has developed further by utilising texts to ascertain the space created by those forms and to view architecture as a cosmological metaphor. With this approach, artistic work and human creation are considered part of a network of collective characteristics that shape the space. Grabar highlights this approach in relation to Baghdad's history: "The true significance of Baghdad lies not so much in the physical character of its forms as in the ideas suggested by the forms".[3]

Among recent attitudes to promote historical understanding is what is outlined by Morkoc, to approach the text from "an experiential perspective that sees architecture as an occasion rather than an object".[4] She suggests when revealing inherent data in such texts, it is more productive to ask dialogic questions rather than to identify the ways in which these historical texts are instrumental in architectural historiography.[5] The experiential perspective suggested by Morkoc is an excellent approach to understand architecture, as it involves other aspects of the architectural experience and does not restrict architectural understanding to physical features only. I assume this approach presents a deeper understanding of history only if dialogic questions follow logical attitudes that aim to extract meaning through scientific means.

It is widely acknowledged that history writings need to be examined carefully, because they may not always present the 'real image'. This is due to the different motives of historians, who may have passed on obscured information. On the other hand, concurrent prose work usually presents many similarities and brings in ideas about the city and the society that cannot be found in other resources. Gadamer highlights the important role of literature, noting "literature is a function of being intellectually preserved and handed down, and therefore brings its hidden history into every age".[6] In the case of Baghdad, texts inherited from different periods of its history contain a wealth of inspiring ideas and perspectives.

Poetry and literature in Baghdad

Baghdad has been home to many famous scholars, who have produced significant intellectual works. Throughout history, it "was a focus of world culture and refinements, where the most distinguished theologians and commentators of Islam . . . were to be found, teaching, discussing and writing".[7] It wasn't only a great centre of theological study, but also a centre for 'more general learning'.[8] While philosophers and theologians debated and discussed scientific matters, poets and writers created some of the greatest works of Arabic literature.[9] In the early centuries of its foundation, Baghdad was unparalleled in the number of bookshops and learning schools.[10] These schools embodied the city's sophisticated literature, linguistic, historical and religious structure. Literature and poetry books had a high ranking and were sold at extensive markets in Baghdad and other Arab cities. Poetry, in particular, is considered 'the treasure of Arabs'[11] and the peak of Arabic literature, since it encompasses such a wealth of ideas.[12]

In Baghdad, history and literature were developed in the eighth century in line with other disciplines such as science, mathematics, chemistry and astronomy. These subjects continued to flourish, as the number of writings increased enormously. Conventional history declares Baghdad's position as a centre of learning weakened after the Mongol invasion in 656/1258. On the contrary, inherited texts from this period assert local scholars carried on scientific research and continued to write attractive literature. The development of new methods in writing, such as *maqāmāt*, is proof of this perseverance. The *maqāmāt* are eloquent, rhymed texts that contain detailed descriptions of events and valuable information about the city and the society. Al-ʾAlusi refers to two exponents of this style in the thirteenth and fourteenth centuries: Ibn al-Sayqal al-Jaziri (d. 701/1301) and Zahir al-din al-Gazaruni al-Baghdadi (d. 697/1297).[13]

The fourteenth century was the start of a massive intellectual movement in Baghdad and other cities in Iraq. At the beginning of this century, scholars realised it was important to protect the city's great heritage of literature, so they undertook the collection of numerous writings on various subjects. Naji reflects on the fourteenth century as "the century of great encyclopedias, scientific writings, and famous historical complications".[14] These encyclopedias, or *mawsūʾāt*, contained huge collections of intellectual writings in different disciplines such as geography, botany, astronomy, history, philology, poetry and literature. Among the scholars who produced these significant writings are Muhammad bin Ibrahim al-ʾAnsari (d. 718/1318), Ahmad bin Yahya al-ʿamri (d. 749/1348), Safiy al-din al-Hilli (d. 750/1349), and Ahmad bin Muhammad al-Tasturi al-Baghdadi (d. 812/1409). Thus, in the fourteenth and fifteenth centuries, Baghdadi scholars continued to produce more written artefacts.

In the sixteenth and seventeenth centuries, the literature movement in Baghdad was affected by two major changes. First, geographical re-distribution resulted in the multiplicity of learning centres in the region, instead of focusing on Baghdad alone. For instance, the city of Hilla[15] gradually grew to become a celebrated learning hub. Second, the noted change of the language utilised in literature influenced the quality of texts. The recurrent invasion of Turkish and Persian forces promoted this change by increasing the number of residents who combined a mix of different nationalities. Instead of considering Arabic the main language for writing, three languages were employed in texts: Turkish, Persian, as well as Arabic. A reasonable number of Arabic writings survived this mix, yet these writings generally focused on prominent people rather than the urban features of the city.

Although scholars continued to write and research in the sixteenth and seventeenth centuries, writings inherited from these centuries are relatively few, due to political instability and the destruction of some learning schools and mosques. This resulted in the loss of a number of these writings, together with a confusion of the identity of the writers. By the mid-seventeenth century, scholars like ʿAli Khan al-Madani (d. 1119/1707) made every effort to collect the prose works of the sixteenth and seventeenth centuries, and they successfully managed to collect a good proportion of precious writings.[16] Subsequently, the Ottoman era contributed to the deterioration of Arabic literature in all Arabic cities under Ottoman control. There was much misuse of language in texts, due to the enforcement of the Turkish language, which not only triggered the growth of slang languages, but also widened the gap between them and pure Arabic.

In the early eighteenth century the cities of Iraq are thought to have lost much of their population. Baghdad, at the end of this century, "numbered perhaps 80,000".[17] The fluctuation in population affected the number of scholars. However, the great amount of poetry and literature produced in this period implies that perhaps the harsh situation was a stimulus for more expressive writing. Cooperson notes "Baghdadi scholars were so numerous and so eminent that reference to them could continue to support the centre of the world book even when the material prosperity and political importance of the city had receded".[18] Unlike deserted monuments or destroyed tributes, intellect is a living structure that can grow and flourish despite ageing and destruction.

In the late eighteenth century, Arabic literature and poetry flourished in Baghdad because of some stability due to the decrease in conquests and the rise in population. As a result, different writings improved and more cultural fora were established, which ensured the regrowth of the original Arabic language. In addition, the founding of printing presses in the first decades of the nineteenth century contributed to the thriving of literature after a period of loss and misuse. Nonetheless, due to the damage that occurred to many books, it is crucial to investigate the originality of the texts that may have been overlapped with time. These issues make the search for original writings in pure Arabic a complicated yet rewarding process for the researcher.

The phenomenon of urban literature

In order to discover the urban qualities of Baghdad in the past, I am implementing 'urban literature' inquiry, which implies examining specific texts to reveal direct connections between place and its social circumstances. The focus is on urban characteristics rather than investigating the entertaining features of literature. Doing so helps define a particular urban culture and allow a broader understanding of history. This type of literature is valuable in recognising the spatial qualities of particular places and their interaction with people. It also identifies the relationships between individuals and society, as "neither the life of an individual nor the history of a society can be understood without understanding both".[19] Cooperson questions the ability of urban literature to draw connections between social circumstances and literary construction, and whether these connections depend on critical definitions of 'urban culture' and 'entertainment literature'.[20] The investigation of urban literature in the next two chapters proves its capability to draw these connections.

As a populist trend in literature, this notion does not normally occupy a large space in current historiographical studies. While the investigation of urban literature aims to understand the life of ordinary individuals to unveil historical meanings, conventional histories generally focus on major events and political leaders of a society. The idea of applying urban literature does not necessarily mean establishing a division in literature that is concerned with urban investigation only, or limiting the study of urban history to urban criteria. It is rather an aid to recognise specific features of the city to establish broader meanings and allow literature to extend to other disciplines, including architecture and urbanism.

Since both poetry and historical narratives reveal plentiful clues about the urban history of Baghdad, both genres are considered valuable sources of urban literature. Although narratives and poems are usually written for certain purposes, when it comes to the city, writings become cohesive with expressive words and affectionate language. This immediacy of poetic language helps to broaden the literary sources used to understand the urban history. The focus on scholars and poets is another advantage of urban literature. Scholars usually stand between common people and political rulers, which makes them an ideal group for interpreting the history of society as a whole.

The language of understanding

Language is a crucial element of expression that affects understanding. The language of writing influences understanding to a great extent. Once the aspects of language are understood collectively, the overall understanding of texts can take place. I call the language that is interpreted systematically 'the language of appreciation', as understanding denotes appreciation. One of the vital features of the Arabic language is its richness through the incorporation of countless words that have diverse and expressive meanings. These qualities make it an ideal poetic language such that "no language on this earth would match it in this character".[21] Another major feature of this language is its connection to the Qur'an, which was revealed in Arabic because no other language had the capacity to convey all the deep meanings that it contained. According to al-Khazraji, all scholars have great debts to the Qur'an, which promoted learning of the sophisticated Arabic language, revealed its beauty and sustained the maximum level of language use.[22]

Awareness of the Qur'an was a crucial prerequisite to any study in the early Islamic era. This understanding required exceptional knowledge of the Arabic language and its modulation. Consequently, philological studies were initiated at an early stage in Islam "due to the importance of philology to the correct recitation of the Qur'an".[23] The Arabic language continued to spread with the expansion of Islam, and it transcended "both regional and tribal considerations".[24] According to al-Duri, grammarians view language from two perspectives: the first regards language as a matter of heritage, and the second sees language in terms of an existing convention and established usage, which necessitates more strictly defined linguistic rules. He states, "Baghdad inherited both of these perspectives".[25]

The outstanding influence of the language of Qur'an was on poetry. The most fascinating poems usually follow the techniques of the Holy Book. Among these techniques is the communication procedure of the Qur'an that uses clarity and conciseness of speech to convey meaning, avoiding long sentences and excessive words. It also introduces the concept of using dialogue and questioning to explain ideas. A third technique used is avoiding explicit statements in order to leave space for thinking, imagining and estimating.[26] Other methods include using opposing words in the same sentence and the surprise element, which is one of the most important stimulating tools of the Qur'an. Yet the most striking method of the Qur'an is the extensive use of metaphors "to help human imagination gain insight into the unseen".[27]

The meaning of texts depends on twofold interpretation: apparent, or literal, interpretation that considers the overt meaning of texts, and the inner or unseen interpretation, which attempts to uncover the concealed meaning of these texts. Al-Saghir explains all words have two linked phenomena: the phonic which refers to their sounds, and the semantic, which refers to their embedded symbolic meaning.[28] He states the relationship between the word and its meaning is twofold, which means that if a term requires a meaning, the meaning will require a term. However, recognising this dual relationship is not sufficient to reveal the full significance of the word because it refers only to the natural property of the word. He points to another property of words that should be considered: the earned property that changes the meaning with time. This property is important because it has links to the historical and psychological aspects of words,[29] which are crucial to their interpretation. This implies the meaning of specific words could change with the passing of time, so it is important to be aware of these changes when analysing urban literature.

On the other hand, instead of focusing on separate words, Taha Hussein focuses on connecting words to establish meaning; since the examination of individual words does not convey full meaning unless these words are interconnected in a creative way that helps to interpret meaning.[30] To achieve this interconnectivity, al-Bustani suggests investigating the geometry of texts by examining the stages of construction and the relationships between all parts, to discover various levels of meaning. This technique makes it simpler to perceive the whole sense of the text ahead of its parts.[31] Moreover, Lankarani notes in addition to the text's literal investigation, we should use intellectual judgement and refer to holy texts to reach a full interpretation.[32] I believe examining single words is important as well as examining the relationships between other parts of the text. Interlocking both procedures establishes a consistent and strong base for a deeper interpretation of texts.

The method of interpretation

The reading of urban literature requires understanding of the language of all texts, which necessitates a method of interpretation. Gadamer suggests different ways to interpret texts:

> Ultimately, whoever interprets poetry can do it from various points of view. He can proceed in the direction of the history of genres by classifying a particular poem among the models of the same literary genre; he can proceed in the direction of the history of motifs; he can extricate the rhetorical and poetic techniques and demonstrate their connection with the structure of the whole, etc. But he can also take upon himself the original hermeneutic task of explaining what is comprehensible.[33]

Gadamer states different techniques of interpretation to achieve understanding, yet he emphasises the hermeneutic task to understand texts. Hermeneutic interpretation that includes critical explanation of texts, philosophy, pragmatics, scriptures, verbal and non-verbal communications can be fruitful to this book's enquiry. This is in contrast to implementing single-sided interpretations, as they only provide a limited level of understanding.

The method 'integrated interpretation' considers all elements of the historical experience and offers a profound understanding of literature. This method puts into practice two major resources: poetry for creative interpretation and historical narratives for social and political analysis. The key objective of this method is to represent different elements collectively and elaborate on how spatial sensibility is presented in these texts, in relation to various architectural, environmental, social, educational and cultural topics. Integrated interpretation constitutes two kinds of interpretation: horizontal and vertical. 'Horizontal interpretation' interprets single words and the whole text, in addition to the comparison between texts, whereas 'vertical interpretation' of texts implies interconnections between texts, the different stages of construction and the comparison between different periods and between various circumstances, allowing the interconnectivity of texts to be recognised.

The outward appearance of a text usually refers to generality, without considering specification, limits and links. Although it is crucial to understand each word, direct horizontal analysis cannot supplement a full understanding of the interlocking aspects of the historical experience. Still, the horizontal level of interpretation is necessary as a basis for any interpretation scheme, but is best used in conjunction with vertical interpretation, to consider all levels of historical development of these texts. While it studies the meaning of the text, it also focuses on their geometry and the dialogue between them, as "a word only becomes a word when it breaks and enters into communicative usage".[34] Undoubtedly the communicative usage of texts reveals meaning, yet the result depends very much on the method of communication. Original texts typically encompass complete meaning, so less communication does not relate to the strength of the text itself; rather, it reflects the insufficiency of modes of interrogation. The comparison between synchronous texts establishes a simple level of understanding, and combining these simple meanings enables construction of composite multiple meanings that takes advantage of the broad usage of words. Hence, the analysis of all simple and multiple meanings with other conventional methods allows us to obtain an advanced level of understanding.

The integrative approach to interpretation enhances intellectual appreciation of identity. This is intimately related to a theoretical network which – through the examination of elements in comparison – clarifies the complexities of history and designates the identity of the city. In addition, a theoretical framework which prevents total separation from divine inspiration strengthens this identity. The method does not view the seen and unseen, which represent contrasting material and spiritual realities, as separate entities. It rather merges these criteria and represents them as interlocked concepts. This method is consistent with Akkach's identification of representation that embraces both the universal and particular.[35] While particular qualities relate to specific norms of society, the representation establishes connections between all elements of history at a universal level.

To denote this method, the analysis in this book juxtaposes the literature and poetry of various writers throughout the history of Baghdad. Through their scholarly works, these writers contribute to the presentation of history, by narrating specific events and expressing their feelings about different conditions. Generally, expressive texts are multidimensional and have a capacity for many dialogic interpretations and few documentary interpretations. These texts usually focus on the symbolic significance of place and metaphoric images rather than describing visible figures. Poetry, in particular, articulates extensive emotional notions such as love and longing and conveys strong connections to place, people, specific traditions and history, while narratives favour visible figures over conceptual metaphoric figures. The interpretation of different stages of the history of texts reveals valuable ideas, and examining these texts collectively embraces both mythical and historical aspects as celebrated insights of the historical experience.

Integrated interpretation implements the presupposition of Gadamer that historical narratives can be used to reveal historical accuracy. Yet, the focus on literature does not imply an idealistic reconstruction of the past. This method advocates literary interpretation as being 'amongst' the major aids to understand history. It also considers conceptual and aesthetic interpretative approaches, which have been the predominant techniques of architectural historiography. Additionally, it recognises simple concepts that multiply and transform gradually into complex concepts. This constant development of ideas is infinite and freed from the limits of time and space. The goal of this approach is to continuously promote advancement of historical narratives, while maintaining connections with the past.

Thematic approach to the interpretation of literature

The measures of the 'integrated interpretation' scheme are applicable to the interpretation of single words and their context, in addition to the whole text. In order to complement further techniques as part of the vertical and horizontal methods of interpretation, I developed the 'thematic approach' that outlines specific themes in the urban literature of Baghdad, to disclose indications of urban life that are hidden in metaphorical compositions. The thematic approach selects a bigger premise and searches for texts that represent a specific theme. It starts by developing a theme in line with a noted absence in historiography and extending it to an overall interpretation of multiple texts, and then approaching specific texts and single words which represent this theme.

Although this approach has the capacity to provide beneficial information, the reverse approach is also fruitful, since both the interpretation of single words and the interpretation of the whole text bring out the meaning of the text. I call this gradual development from the single meaning of multiple texts to multiple meanings 'cumulative approach', which is part of a twofold interpretation. However, 'thematic approach' seems more appropriate for this inquiry, since it frees texts from limited interpretation and provides compound ideas rather than the literal meaning of single words. The suggested themes are centred on some powerful observations that comprise emotional expressions such as love, attachment, happiness, beauty, grief and pride. These expressions are indicated in literature in relation to many spatial themes.

An overall reading of these texts reveals love as the most compelling motive in the history of Baghdad. In general, the love of a place, of people and ideas, is the most powerful and influential matter in life. It dictates human behaviour, perception and interaction with others and contributes to the formation of cities. These matters are discussed in relation to the interconnections of writers with different urban spaces. I have classified these themes into three categories, in reference to the nature of the topics that group them together. The first group is 'spatial themes' that relate to particular characteristics of urban space. The second group includes 'nostalgic themes', which comprises themes of love, attachment, beauty, happiness and social relations. The third group relates to 'reflective themes' that are revealed through external observations by people who visit the place. The aim of classifying these three themes is to simplify their presentation, while realising their interlocking aspects. The interconnection between various contexts represented in the three themes assists in reconceptualising history through coherent meanings.

Notes

1 Morkoc, 'Reading architecture from the text', p. 47.
2 Morkoc, *A study of Ottoman narratives on architecture*, p. 18.
3 Grabar, *The formation of Islamic art*, p. 69.
4 Morkoc, 'Reading architecture from the text', p. 38.
5 Morkoc, 'Reading architecture from the text', p. 47.
6 Gadamer, *Truth and method*, p. 161.
7 Smith, *An early mystic of Baghdad*, p. 60.
8 Lassner, *The topography of Baghdad in the early middle ages*, p. 17.
9 'Abdullah, *Merchants, Mamluks and murder*, p. 9.
10 Ma'ruf, 'al-ḥayāt al-thaqāfiyya fī Baghdad', p. 168.
11 Al-Khazraji, 'taqāsīm al-qafza al-'adabiyya'.
12 Al-Khazraji, 'taqāsīm al-qafza al-'adabiyya'.
13 Al-'Alusi, *Baghdad fī al-shi'r al-'arabī*, p. 150.
14 Naji, 'simāt al-'aṭà al-fikrī fī al-qarn al-thāmin al-hijrī'.
15 This city is situated 100 kilometres south of Baghdad.
16 Shubbar, *'adab al-ṭaff*, p. 9.
17 Inalcik & Quataert, *An economic and social history of the Ottoman Empire*, p. 654.

18 Cooperson, 'Baghdad in rhetoric and narrative', pp. 99–113.
19 Mills, *The social imagination*, p. 3.
20 Cooperson, 'Baghdad in rhetoric and narrative', pp. 99–113.
21 Said & Suleiman, *The Arabs today*, p. 27.
22 Al-Khazraji, 'taqāsīm al-qafza al-'adabiyya'.
23 Al-Duri, *The historical formation of the Arab nation*, p. 88.
24 Al-Duri, *The historical formation of the Arab nation*, p. 46.
25 Al-Duri, *The historical formation of the Arab nation*, p. 89.
26 Al-Saghir, '*taṭawwur al-baḥth al-dalālī fī al-Qur'an al-karīm*', pp. 22–24.
27 Akkach, *Cosmology and architecture in pre-modern Islam*, p. 30.
28 Al-Saghir, '*taṭawwur al-baḥth al-dalālī fī al-Qur'an al-karīm*', p. 16.
29 Al-Saghir, '*taṭawwur al-baḥth al-dalālī fī al-Qur'an al-karīm*', p. 21.
30 Al-Saghir, '*taṭawwur al-baḥth al-dalālī fī al-Qur'an al-karīm*', p. 22.
31 Al-Bustani, *al-tafsīr al-binā'i li al-Qur'an al-karīm*.
32 Lankarani, *madkhal al-tafsīr*.
33 Gadamer, *Literature and philosophy in dialogue*, p. 153.
34 Gadamer, 'Language and understanding', pp. 13–27.
35 Akkach, *Cosmology and architecture in pre-modern Islam*, p. 162.

3 The urban literature of Baghdad before the eighteenth century

Representing the round city

In this chapter, I will examine the urban literature of Baghdad since the foundation of the round city until the eighteenth century. Thematic approach is applied in relation to the urban history of Baghdad prior to the eighteenth century, along with the principles of 'vertical interpretation' that imply investigation of all phases in history. I will start with the prose composed since the foundation of the round city until it was deserted and ruined over time. The representation of the round city mainly focuses on spatial themes, since nostalgic and reflective themes were hardly expressed in the writings of this period. The short phase of this city, its unappealing social conditions, and the negative aspects that accompanied its foundation may explain the reason of the shortage of nostalgic and reflective themes in literature. Unlike current historical accounts of the round city that highlight its thriving qualities, the texts of the ninth century contain few indications of its prosperous material qualities. In contrast, these texts reflect social and economic issues, which suggests gradual reduction of spatial qualities.

Among the situations that are indicated in the poems of that period is that of unequal distribution of wealth. People were extremely poor, and life was exceedingly expensive. Meanwhile, palaces were built with bolts made from gold and silver, and with gardens containing rare plants and amazing features.[1] The famous poet 'abu al-'Atahiyya (d. 213/826) wrote a poem complaining about the rise in prices while tax money was heavily collected:

> Who can tell the caliph my continuous advices?
> I see the prices are extremely high
> And job opportunities are few and poverty is increasing
> And the orphans and the widows live in empty houses[2]

This poem indicates that although the physical structure of the round city was impressive, people did not enjoy living there because of the economic problems. It also shows an overlooked spatial quality of this city, presented in the empty houses of the poor, and suggests the existence of two opposite social situations of wealth and poverty in this city, unlike conventional writings that suggest wealth as the only remarkable condition of that era.

Another poem by 'Ali al-Talibi outlines other problems in the city. The round city experienced a siege in 196/811 which caused damage to some parts of the city. Al-Talibi expresses sympathy with the dramatic consequences of that siege, and he associates these problems with injustice, breakdown in relations between relatives and the negligent attitude of scholars. He declares that the weakening of the city's position resulted from an increase of bad deeds that shortened its life:

> The strong bonds between relatives and tribes are cut
> And educated and pious people did not intervene
> This destruction is a revenge from Allah and a punishment for those
>   people
> For the hefty sins they committed[3]

These lines reveal another spatial quality represented in the interrelationship between human bonds, the level of education and the intensity of destruction. They highlight the great influence of social and cultural matters on the material conditions of the city. This emphasises the need to interpret poetry to disclose more factual aspects of urban history that do not necessarily relate to political matters.

The gradual moving of residents outside the city changed the physical conditions of the round city dramatically. These changes are depicted in the poem of 'Omara bin Aqil bin Bilal al-Khatafi, who lived in Basra, a city south of Baghdad. He visited Baghdad after the abandoning of the round city[4] and wrote reflective texts. His poems indicate the constantly fluctuating character of Baghdad, denoted in the contradictory conditions of prosperity and construction on one side, and damage and destruction on the other. Al-Khatafi expresses little grief about the destruction of the round city, but admires both the physical and religious structures of the city.

> There is nothing like Baghdad in both material and spiritual attributes
> Yet its conditions are unsteady and keep changing from time to time[5]

These terms indicate the mixed feelings he experienced on the damaged round city and the flourishing second settlement. The poet relates the changing conditions of Baghdad to both material and spiritual attributes, which suggests an equal influence of these qualities on each other and on the condition of the city.

The analysis of these three poems helps establish a view about the round city as a temporary component of the history of Baghdad that exhibits contrasting notions of privilege and adversity. Unlike conventional sources, these texts do not emphasise the material splendour of this city, nor do they extend this historical interpretation to the whole city of Baghdad. Actually, these texts reveal more negative issues than positive issues, which shows the significance of social matters in the general understanding of the city.

The second settlement of Baghdad: spatial themes

Unlike the first settlement (round city), the second settlement of Baghdad that was built on both sides of the Tigris River is presented greatly in the urban literature of that period. The great number of texts enable a thorough representation that implements the thematic approach by focussing on each theme separately. These themes are often interlocking in texts, which further enriches the meaning. The texts that presented spatial themes of the second settlement of Baghdad reveal astonishment at features of greenery and the loveliness of the river, in addition to outstanding architectural elements. Although the architectural components of Baghdad were highly admired in such literature, it seems that the proximity of this settlement to the Tigris River amplified perception of the city's beauty. This characteristic became a quality of Baghdad constantly echoed in different texts throughout Baghdad's history. The integration of natural and architectural beauty created a magnificent picture that was esteemed by visitors and residents alike. The poet al-Khatafi[6] expresses a gorgeous image of the expanded settlements outside the round city:

> Between the farms of Qaṭrabul[7] and *al-karkh* there are fields of narcissus flowers
> And there is every fine plant and fragrant flower
> You see *dijla* [Tigris River] and its streams everywhere in this land
> With many ships racing like horses
> And there you find inviting palaces that embrace you with wings
> Those attributes attract and welcome all visitors to the place[8]

This poem paints a magnificent picture of the second settlement of Baghdad and expresses happiness and comfort on both sides of the river. The natural environment of the river, the large castles on its shores and the amazing greenery of the surrounding farms contributed to this boundless expression of beauty. The poet describes remarkable qualities of the architecture of the palaces that allowed them to communicate with people and invite them in. This indicates that specific architectural forms can promote interaction between people and place. These qualities are worthy of investigation in further studies.

The geographer, Shams al-din al-Bashari al-Maqdisi (d. 380/990), who was born in Jerusalem, toured almost all cities in the Islamic world. He depicted a beautiful picture of the second settlement of Baghdad in his narratives. In addition to architectural and natural assets, he connected the splendour of place to social beauty, by describing the humour, talent and knowledge of the people of Baghdad:

> Baghdad has pleasant and charming qualities for its inhabitants. These qualities include humour, talent, friendliness and knowledge. Its air is gentle and its scientific approaches are accurate. It contains every excellence and beauty. Intellectual people are born there, and all hearts are attached to Baghdad. This city is complete and famous, and above any description or praise.[9]

In this statement, al-Bashari juxtaposes spatial qualities, such as gentle air, with intellectual scientific thinking. He refers to distinctive social qualities that resulted from this juxtaposition, comprising humour, sociability and knowledge. These qualities are collectively highlighted as entities of the complete beauty of Baghdad, which was the main reason for the geographer's affection to the city. He refers to social beauty as part of the city's collective beauty rather than admiring it separately, which signifies the equal significance of spiritual and social qualities. Despite the fact that al-Bashari visited Baghdad more than a hundred years after al-Khatafi's visit, he also indicated the prosperity of the city in his writing. In contrast to al-Khatafi's remarks, al-Bashari was amazed by the social beauty and the natural environment more than the architectural magnificence, despite the fact that Baghdad still had great mansions at that time.

These observations suggest advanced scientific thought, and the numerous learning institutes that were founded continually created a new dimension of beauty – the social educational dimension. This new element dominated the conception of beauty at that time, and was therefore echoed in the urban literature of the tenth century. Yet, all writings in this period agreed on the place's natural beauty as the most fixed variable of attractiveness. The literature of late thirteenth and fourteenth centuries also associates spatial and environmental qualities with social qualities. I quote parts of *maqāmāt* by al-Gazaruni (d. 697/1297):

> I swear by God that I have never seen a city better than Baghdad. How can someone dare to find a similar place! Can he compare the foot with the head? . . . The Hajj season is one of the great seasons in the year . . .

People move happily in the gardens of the western side of *dijla*. Decorated tents are established to feed those who spend days celebrating as individuals and as groups. When the Hajj caravan arrives, the roads will open to the pilgrims who are treated like brides and grooms, and transported to their homes in procession . . . And sometimes people set out to the stunning gardens to see the beautiful flowers and hear the songs of the blackbirds . . . In spring time, people gather and assemble near the streams, and they filter through the surrounding trees. They collect fruit from trees, and they spread out on the grass and on the flowers in the farm.[10]

Al-Gazaruni points out a number of events, and presents them in connection with impressive spatial qualities, including the river and the gardens. He describes bright days of the past, and elaborates various occasions such as Hajj season, fasting season, cemetery season,[11] weekly outings and spring time. These show the pleasure experienced in Baghdad during different religious or climatic seasons, and portray the western side of the city as an open area that had more capacity for recreation than the eastern side, with plenty of beautiful gardens and streams.

After the fourteenth century, direct spatial references became less frequent in literature and poetry, suggesting the influence of unstable conditions on the objectives of writings. Yet, the texts indirectly described exotic architectural forms. The literature of this period up to the eighteenth century presented an outstanding aspect that shows less political intimation, and more focus on the social aspects. The period between the fifteenth and eighteenth centuries encouraged more historical writing to sustain the relationships with the honourable history of the city. These writings inspired people to improve social affairs and to sustain a decent life. The strong appreciation of the city regardless of its fluctuating conditions indicates the great effect of social qualities on the development and continuity of the city.

The second settlement of Baghdad: nostalgic themes

The reading of urban literature shows that the second settlement of Baghdad evoked greater contrasting emotions. While the city's wonderful attributes were articulated by visitors, residents found it hard to continue living there in the eleventh century. Mounting economic problems and the shortage of funds compelled some residents of Baghdad to travel far away for their livelihoods. Among those people was the poet ibn Zurayq al-Baghdadi (d. 420/1029). This poet was born in Baghdad, but because of the insufficiency of basic needs for his family, he decided to travel to Andalusia for a better life. He never returned to Baghdad because he became ill and died in Andalusia. Al-Baghdadi remained depressed while he was away from his birthplace. He expressed his grief in a poem, stating no other city could substitute for Baghdad and no other people could replace the people of Baghdad:

> I left Baghdad and its people, aiming to find a comparable place
> But I realised that I decided on something that leads to hopelessness
> It is impossible to find a better place!
> For me Baghdad is 'the entire world'
> And the residents of Baghdad are 'all of humankind'[12]

Al-Baghdadi's remarks point out the suffering of being away from Baghdad, despite the problems there, and show that natural beauty, connections and educational development added to this pain. Economic hardship was also one of the most powerful impressions of the place, capable of influencing other measures of happiness. Soon after his departure from the city, the poet expressed a metaphoric meaning of Baghdad; stating that Baghdad is the world for him, and the people of Baghdad represent humankind. These nostalgic expressions suggest that difficult times did not change people's perception of Baghdad. They also suggest the strong relationship between material and social influences on the overall context of the city in literature.

Among the unique aspects of Baghdad in the tenth and eleventh centuries was the great number of universities and schools that attracted knowledgeable people everywhere, who considered it a merit to visit Baghdad at some stage of their life. The relatively easy immigration, and the urgent need for teachers, encouraged many scholars to reside in Baghdad permanently. Yet sometimes the shortage of funds affected their decision to stay there. For example, the poet and philosopher abu al-ʿAlaʾ al-Maʿarri (d. 449/1057) stayed in Baghdad for a while. He was teaching there, and participating in cultural debates, but experienced a shortage of funds. He wrote some poems blaming the treasurer of *dār al-ʿilm* (the science centre) in Baghdad.

> The cause that made me leave Baghdad is the same cause that deluded Adam and Eve
> And got them down to earth from the grand paradise[13]

The lack of supplies forced al-Maʿarri to leave Baghdad, sadly. He likened his trip out of Baghdad to the separation of Adam and Eve from paradise, which indicates the huge loss he felt when he left the city, and the excessive beauty of Baghdad that evoked images of paradise in his imagination.

Al-Maʿarri wrote another poem expressing his great attachment to Baghdad and its people, whom he loved and considered as his family:

> Oh people of Baghdad, I bid farewell to you
> And my entire body keeps stinging and burning from inside due to my sadness
> I consider *sham* [Syria] and its people the worse substitution to Baghdad and Baghdadis
> However, they continue to be my people and their place remains my homeland
> Can someone provide me with a sip of water from *dijla*?
> I would gulp all the water of *dijla* if it was possible[14]

This poem exhibits an extraordinary attachment to Baghdad by a visitor, who expressed much pain of leaving the city, due to economic hardship. Nevertheless, it seems as though there was a considerable improvement in the economic situation in the late eleventh century, at least for the teaching scholars. The eminent scholar al-Ghazali arrived at Baghdad in 484/1091 and he commended the financial system in *al-madrasa al-nizamiyya* where he stayed and taught:

> The wealth of Iraq was available for good works, since it constitutes a trust fund for the benefit of Muslims. Nowhere in the world have I seen better financial arrangements to assist a scholar to provide for his children.[15]

The attachment to Baghdad expressed in al-Maʿarri's poem, and favouring it over his homeland, shows how social, cultural and natural attributes establish attractive places for visitors and residents alike. In addition to expressing love and affection to the city as a whole, al-Maʿarri indicated particular attachment to the Tigris River and its water. This suggests the significance of some urban features of the city in the understanding of its history. It also suggests the benefit of interpreting poetry through the thematic approach.

By the mid-thirteenth century, the Mongols raided Baghdad and put an end to the Abbasid era. As discussed, conventional historiography proposes that this event marked a sharp end to an era of prosperity and established the start of a period of recurrent disasters and conflicts. On the other hand, the literature of this period continued in the same manner of double meanings and varying expressions, which implies the inappropriateness of such definitive conclusions. It appears that social beauty experienced a slight setback in this period due to the loss of some scholars and the damage to learning centres. The reading of texts suggests the terrible situation after the Mongol invasion did not last for centuries, as shown in conventional histories. It rather shows that the situation improved by the end of the thirteenth century, when the Mongols were defeated in the battle of ʿayn Jalut in 658/1260 and lost control by 690/1292.[16]

Literature proves the continuity of the city as an attractive learning centre that maintained its natural and social beauties despite troubles. The literature of the thirteenth and fourteenth centuries gained a new element of remembrance and sadness. It is worth noting that such an element in literature did not occur after the destruction of the round city, which suggests less attachment of people to the round city. Conversely, this practice emerged in literature after the invasion of the Mongols in 656/1258, indicating greater appreciation of the qualities of the second settlement of Baghdad. With the frequent unpredictable events that took place in Baghdad in subsequent centuries, this practice of beginning with sorrowful expressions continued until the eighteenth and nineteenth centuries, along with other aspects such as appreciation of the natural and social beauties of the place. The poem of shaykh Shams al-din Mahmud al-Hashimi (d. 675/ 1276) is a good example of this trend:

> If my tears did not make my eyelids filled with wounds
> After you passed away, then I am packed with antipathy
> I wonder what happened to those homes and why everything
>   has changed
> Where are my beloved ones and where are my old neighbours?
> After my beloved people left, I wish that no breeze would pass here
> And no flower would blossom and no tree branch would
>   swing happily[17]

Al-Hashimi depicts the devastating conditions after the Mongol invasion, and expresses deep sadness about losing good friends and neighbours. Although the city maintained its natural beauty, this single measure of relief did not heal his wounds which, instead, stemmed from the lack of social measures. This investigation suggests that nostalgic themes are also powerful tools that promote the understanding of various aspects of the history of Baghdad. Unlike remembrance that relates meanings to the past, nostalgic themes represent the past effectively and promote its interaction with the present to improve historical understanding.

The second settlement of Baghdad: reflective themes

The reading of Baghdad's history through different eras indicates the continual movement of scholars between it and other cities in the region. The informal means of relocation, the attractive character of Baghdad and the changing conditions of the city triggered these constant relocations. These circumstances stimulated affection and attachment to the city. Being in a much admired and honoured city such as Baghdad gave the scholars a sense of pride and integrity, even for those who only visited for a short period of time. Consequently, social and educational variables continued to develop until they dominated other measurements. The poet al-Ma'arri was among the scholars who were amazed at the qualities of Baghdad and dreamt of visiting it and staying there. Al-Ma'arri was born in Ma'arra near Aleppo in 363/973. He had longed to visit Baghdad since his teens but couldn't make it until he was 36. In 398/1007, al-Ma'arri reached Baghdad and found it to be a gathering place for philosophers and theologians from different cultures. He was intrigued by the city's natural beauties, and so wrote a poem appreciating the river and trees in a similar way to the learning institutes of Baghdad:

> We were longing for Iraq while we were in our early youth
> But we couldn't get there until we became middle-aged
> We drank the finest, pure water from *dijla*
> And we visited the palm trees which are the noblest trees[18]

Al-Ma'arri expressed extreme longing for Baghdad, which he referred to as Iraq. This was because Baghdad was the site of the central government, and a visitor to Baghdad was regarded as a visitor to Iraq. This was a common impression then. For example, when al-Ghazali resided in Baghdad about a century later, he was called imam al-Iraq. Al-Ma'arri describes the water of *dijla* as the best water.[19] Although the fine taste of this water was also indicated in the writings of other poets, it seems as though, for him, the taste of this water was unique, as it was mixed with his emotions and his great admiration of Baghdad. Al-Ma'arri specifies the water of *dijla* as clean, pure water, and considers it among the appealing elements of the city, which evoked attachment and familiarity with the place regardless of the poet's original homeland.

The poem of al-Ma'arri shows how the glory of high level of education turned the natural features of Baghdad, such as the Tigris River and palm trees, into valuable symbolic icons. However, it appears the astonishing picture of Baghdad drawn by al-Ma'arri changed in the twelfth century. The poet ibn al-Ta'awidhi (d. 553/1158) visited Baghdad about a century after al-Ma'arri's visit. His poem shows an increase in social and economic problems, such as injustice and inequity:

> If you intend to visit Baghdad then turn away from it
> As this place is full of oppression and injustice
> If you have desires in Baghdad I advise you to go back
> Because all doors are closed to people's demands[20]

In this poem, al-Taʿawidhi refers to injustice and inequity in wealth distribution, experienced in the twelfth century. He did not mention the natural beauties of the city, which shows how perceptions are changeable in the minds of writers and how they are interrelated with other aspects of the city, paralleling political and economic phases. These changes inclined people to leave the city, though Baghdad intermittently continued to attract scholars to live there. Among these scholars is the poet and religious scholar Safiy al-din al-Hilli, who was among the many eminent scholars of the fourteenth century. Al-Hilli was born in 675/1276 in Hilla. He lived in various cities including Baghdad, Damascus, Cairo and Mardin, yet he stayed for the longest time in Baghdad and died there in 750/1349.

Historians consider al-Hilli's eloquent poems among the foremost products of Arabic literature from that century, as he initiated new methods of arts, poetry and literature that had not been practiced before.[21] Among the particular objectives of the poems of al-Hilli, and of other scholars at that time, is their advice to keep remembering God and His power, and to appreciate His blessings to avoid distress. These poems demonstrate the great influence that scholars had on people throughout the history of Baghdad, and their immense role in calming anxiety and helping people to rise above their problems. For example, al-Hilli wrote a poem advising people to avoid centring their thinking on problems, and to keep hoping for the best, as a productive manner of overcoming the troubles of life:

> Turn away from your worries
> And leave things to your destiny
> Maybe narrow ways will suddenly expand
> And maybe open wide spaces will become narrow[22]

Al-Hilli explains that good and bad situations will never remain endless, as hard times might get better, and good things could get worse. He associates spatial qualities, such as size and narrowness, with feelings and emotions, emphasising the strong influence of various emotions on the conception of place. These juxtaposed characteristics are important techniques to understand the past, as material scales and measurements cannot present the real conditions of the city unless they are linked to other immaterial qualities. Baghdad was not al-Hilli's home city, yet his poems imply his enthusiasm and pride for it and its people. Another poem associates love and pride of Baghdad with high ethics and social relationships. Al-Hilli conveys his views about a battle that took place in Baghdad, which proves the courage and nobility of his group. It also illustrates strong connections between his people and high ethical standards, indicating the appreciation of good values in society and the association of these values with the remarkable history of the city:

> I recall that day when a battle took place in *al-zawra* ' of Iraq
> When we defeated our enemies like they used to defeat us
> We are a nation of high ethics and nobility
> We don't hurt anyone first until he hurts us
> Our deeds are white, our battles are black
> Our farms are green, and our swords are red[23]

This poem reflects a double interaction between place and people. Al-Hilli conveys pride in Baghdad, recollecting its bright history by referring to it as *al-zawra* ' of Iraq.[24] He employs a technique from the Qur'an of using opposing words in comparison with each other. He also utilises the symbolic meanings of colours to explain specific features of the city. While he highlights the farms of Baghdad with the green colour that symbolises fertility, he relates their deeds to white colour that symbolises purity and nobility. On the other hand, he associates their battles with black colour to symbolise their bravery, and their swords with red to symbolise victory. The continuous renewal of writing methods in the fourteenth century indicates remarkable development in different branches of knowledge, despite fluctuating conditions. These styles in literature continued to develop through the fifteenth century. On the other hand, the literature of the sixteenth and seventeenth centuries reflected influences from a combination of multiple languages, which reduced Arabic writings to an extent.

In the literature of the sixteenth century onwards, notions of Sufism started to appear and they grew rapidly in the region. Among the eminent Sufi Iraqi poets in the sixteenth century was Muhammad bin Sulayman Fuḍuli al-Baghdadi.[25] In addition to Sufi prayers and reflections, his poems focused on praising the companions of Prophet Muhammad, advising people to be positive and withstand any terrible situations that faced them:

> I am proud of the love and passion that are hidden inside me
> This is a blessing from Allah which is granted to whomever He
>   chooses
> Without Him being the centre of all eras
> The system of the universe would be disturbed[26]

Fuduli's poems were powerful, as they contributed vastly to the restoration of positive values in society.[27] These poems indicated love and appreciation of the city and its society, but they were not focused on physical descriptions. Instead, they were filled with emotional appeals to God's mercy in order to obtain strength and hope. Another literary objective of the sixteenth century was travel writings, as many scholars had a passion for travel to learn about different cities in the region. An example of these writings is *al-rihla al-abbāsiyya* by Mustafa 'abd al-Qadir al-Abbasi (d. 971/1563).[28] The writing of history was also another remarkable objective of literature in this century, and in the centuries following. The book *tārīkh Baghdad* (history of Baghdad) by Ma'mun bin Bega (997/1588)[29] is an example of such historical references.[30]

Moreover, the sixteenth century produced a great number of collected anthologies by various poets. An example of these books is *gulcan shu'arā* by Ahmad bin Shams al-Baghdadi (d. 1002/1593).[31] The writing methods of the sixteenth century continued to exist in the seventeenth century. These include collecting anthologies by various poets, documenting historical events and travel writing. An example of a major reference for the poets of the seventeenth century is the book *khizānat al-'adab* (rhetoric treasures)[32] by 'abd al-Qadir bin 'Umar al-Baghdadi (d. 1093/1682).[33] Additionally, the book *'uyūn 'akhbār al-'a'yān* (history of famous scholars) by Ahmad bin 'abd Allah al-Baghdadi al-Ghurabi (d. 1102/1690) is an example of historical books that comprised extensive research about Islamic history[34] (Figure 3.1). These modes in literature continued to develop in the first half of the eighteenth century. An example of these books is the significant book about the history of Baghdad called *gulcan khulafā* (history of caliphs).[35]

The ample quantity of writings at these times asserts that intellectual movements were not heavily affected by political conflicts,[36] yet these conflicts occasionally caused a reduction in such products. The representation of Baghdad since its foundation shows an inconsistent yet plentiful amount of intellectual writings. The textual representation illustrated a distinctive phenomenon in Baghdad's literature, which was the enhancement of remembrance as a common method in writing. The period between the establishment of Baghdad and the eighteenth century introduced numerous writings on different subjects. Unlike the poetry of the period between the tenth and fourteenth centuries, which contained direct clues on the urban forms of Baghdad, the texts between the fifteenth and eighteenth centuries lacked these direct indications. However, literature continued to convey different spatial and nostalgic ideas. The reading of these texts confirms the disparity between political and intellectual lines in history, regardless of their intermittent influence.

Figure 3.1 A page in a book by Ahmad al-Ghurabi

Source: Ra'uf (2009).

Notes

1 Al-ʾAlusi, *Baghdad fī al-shiʿr al-ʿarabī*, p. 77.
2 Al-ʾAlusi, *Baghdad fī al-shiʿr al-ʿarabī*, p. 95. The Arabic script:

من مبلغ عنّي الأمام   نصائحا متوالية
اني أرى الأسعار   أسعار الرعيّة غالية
وأرى المكاسب نزرة   وأرى الضّرورة فاشية
وأرى اليتامى والأرامل   في البيوت الخالية

3 Al-ʾAlusi, *Baghdad fī al-shiʿr al-ʿarabī*, p. 114. The Arabic script:

تقطّعت الأرحام بين العشائر   وأسلمهم أهل التّقى والبصائر
فذاك انتقام الله من خلقه بهم   لما اجترموه من عظيم الكبائر

4 Al-Khatafi visited the whole area of Baghdad which comprises both settlements (the round city on the west side of the Tigris River, and the second settlement on the east side of the river). In some historical writings, both settlements are called Baghdad, which adds more confusion to the history of Baghdad.
5 Al-ʾAlusi, *Baghdad fī al-shiʿr al-ʿarabī*, p. 22. The Arabic script:

ما مثل بغداد في الدّنيا ولا الدين   على تقلّبها في كلّ ما حين

6 Al-Khatafi remained alive until the time of the caliph al-Wathiq (d. 232/847).
7 Qaṭrabul was one of the districts in the area of Baghdad to the west of the Tigris River.
8 Al-ʾAlusi, *Baghdad fī al-shiʿr al-ʿarabī*, pp. 22–23. The Arabic script:

مابين قطربل والكرخ نرجسة   تندى ومنبت خيريّ ونسرين
تستنّ دجلة فيما بينها فترى   دهم السّفين تعالى كالبراذين
فيها القصور التي تهوي بأجنحة   بالزائرين الى القوم المزورين

9 Al-ʾAlusi, *Baghdad fī al-shiʿr al-ʿarabī*, p. 22. The Arabic script:

"بغداد لأهلها الخصائص والظّرافة. والقرائح واللّطافة. هواء رقيق وعلم دقيق, كل جيّد بها, وكل حسن فيها, وكل حاذق منها, وكل قلب اليها. وهي أشهر من أن توصف , وأحسن من أن تنعت, وأعلى من أن تمدح"

10 Al-ʾAlusi, *Baghdad fī al-shiʿr al-ʿarabī*, pp. 152–153. The Arabic script:

"وحقّك لا والله. ما نظرت عيني الى أحسن منها الى بلدة أبدا, وكيف يمثّل بها أو يقاس, أويشبّه بالقدم الراس؟ . . . موسم الحج وهو أعظم مواسم السّنة. . . تضرب على دجلة الحياض والروايا. . يرتعون في رياض الجانب الغربي . . . فلايزالون كذلك أياما يمرحون وحدانا وفئاما, والسّبل تجلى في الموكب الى الخيام. وتزف الى منازلها . . . ومنها أعياد ومواسم . . يخرج النّاس الى الرّياض والأزاهير لسماع أصوات الشّحارير . . . وأما زمن الربيع. . فأنهم كانوا يصطحبون ويتجمّعون. . . ويدخلون نهر عيسى. . . فيخترقون أشجاره, ويقطفون ثماره ونواره, ويفترشون رياضه وأزهاره"

11 The cemetery season refers to a specific time when people used to visit the graveyards of their relatives and beloved ones.
12 Al-ʾAlusi, *Baghdad fī al-shiʿr al-ʿarabī*, p. 23. The Arabic script:

سافرت أبغي لبغداد وساكنها   مثلا، قد اخترت شيئا دونه الياس
هيهات ! بغداد الدنيا بأجمعها   عندي، وسكان بغداد هم الناس

13 Al-ʾAlusi, *Baghdad fī al-shiʿr al-ʿarabī*, p. 123. The Arabic script:

وماسار بي الا الذي غر آدما   وحوّاء حتى أدرك الشّرف الهبط

14 Al-ʾAlusi, *Baghdad fī al-shiʿr al-ʿarabī*, p. 121. The Arabic script:

اودّعكم ياأهل بغداد والحشا   على زفرات ماينين من اللّذع
فبئس البديل الشّام منكم وأهله   على أنّهم قومي وبينهم ربعي
ألا زوّدوني شربة ولو انّني   قدرت اذن أفنيت دجلة بالجرع

15 Kritzeck, *Anthology of Islamic literature*, p. 190.
16 Naji, 'simāt al-ʿaṭà al-fikrī fī al-qarn al-thāmin al-ḥijrī', p. 191.
17 Al-ʾAlusi, *Baghdad fī al-shiʿr al-ʿarabī*, pp. 145–147. The Arabic script:

ان لم تقرّح أدمعي أجفاني   من بعد بعدكم فما أجفاني
ما للمنازل أصبحت لا أهلها   أهلي ولا جيرانها جيراني
سرتم فلا سرت النسيم ولازها   زهر ولا ماست غصون البان

18 Al-ʾAlusi, *Baghdad fī al-shiʿr al-ʿarabī*, p. 120. The Arabic script:

كلفنا بالعراق ونحن شرخ   فلم نلمم به الا كهولا
وردنا ماء دجلة خير ماء   وزرنا أشرف الشّجر النّخيلا

19 It is worthy of note the second river that passes through Iraq, the Euphrates River, also passes through Syria or *bilād al-shām*, al-Maʿarri's home. Yet he was longing to taste Tigris River water because of its symbolic aspects.
20 Al-ʾAlusi, *Baghdad fī al-shiʿr al-ʿarabī*, p. 127. The Arabic script:

ياقاصدا بغداد حد عن بلدة   للجور فيها زخرة وعباب
ان كنت طالب حاجة فارجع فقد   سدّت على الراجي بها الأبواب

21 Al-Zarkali, *al-aʿalām*.
22 Al-Bustani, *dīwān safiy al-dīn al-ḥilli*. The Arabic script:

كن عن همومك معرضا   وكل الأمور الى القضا
فلربما اتّسع المضيق   وربما ضاق الفضا

23 Al-Bustani, *dīwān safiy al-dīn al-ḥilli*, pp. 20–21. The Arabic script:

يايوم وقعة زوراء العراق وقد   دنّا الأعادي كما كانوا يدينونا
انا لقوم أبت أخلاقنا شرفا   أن نبتدي بالأذى من ليس يؤذينا
بيض صنائعنا سود وقائعنا   خضر مرابعنا حمر مواضينا

24 The name *al-zawrà* refers to the round city of Baghdad. Yet it appears that the second settlement of Baghdad also inherited this powerful historical name.
25 This poet was born in Karbalà (an Iraqi city, about 105 kilometres south-east of Baghdad) in 887/1483. Later, he moved to Hilla where he resided for some time, before moving to Baghdad. Lastly, he moved back to Karbalà, where he died during a plague epidemic in 963/1556. Fuḍuli composed eloquent poems in three languages; Arabic, Turkish and Persian, and was proud that he did not leave Iraq at any stage of his life.
26 Bayat, *Fuḍuli al-Baghdadi: shaʿir ʾahl al-Bayt*, <www.bizturkmeniz.com/ar/showArticle.asp?id=13397>. The Arabic script:

اباهي بوجد قد تكمّن في الحشا   وذلك فضل الله يؤتيه من يشا
فلولا مدار الدهر مركز خاله   لكان نظام الكائنات مشوّشا

27 Oghlu, *Fuḍuli al-Baghdadi*.
28 Rảuf, *al-tārikh wa al-muʾarrikhūn al-ʿirāqiyyūn*, p. 109.
29 Rảuf, *al-tārikh wa al-muʾarrikhūn al-ʿirāqiyyūn*, p. 113.

30 This book took the form of a diary, which comprised broad descriptions of the different governments of Baghdad.

31 Ràuf, *al-tārikh wa al-mu'arrikhūn al-'irāqiyyūn*, p. 114.

32 Ràuf, *al-tārikh wa al-mu'arrikhūn al-'irāqiyyūn*, p. 126.

33 Additionally, the book *'uyūn 'akhbār al-'a'yān* by Ahmad bin 'abd Allah al-Baghdadi al-Ghurabi (d. 1102/1690) is an example of historical books that comprised extensive research about Islamic history. A third example of the literature of the seventeenth century is a travel book written by Muhammad bin 'abd al-Hamid al-Baghdadi (d. 1064/1653), who travelled to many cities including Baghdad, Makkah, Aleppo and Damascus. (Ràuf, *al-tārikh wa al-mu'arrikhūn al-'irāqiyyūn*, pp. 131–133).

34 Ràuf, *al-tārikh wa al-mu'arrikhūn al-'irāqiyyūn*, pp. 132–133.

35 This book is written by Murtada 'al Nazmi (d. 1136/1732). Ràuf, *al-tārikh wa al-mu'arrikhūn al-'irāqiyyūn*, p. 140.

36 Other distinctive scholars of this period are Muhammad Amin al-Kazimi (d. 1118/1706), who wrote many books relating to history and to Arabic literature, and Yusuf 'Aziz al-Mawlawi (d. 1153/1740) who was a poet, a historian and a Sufi leader. (Ràuf, *al-tārikh wa al-mu'arrikhūn al-'irāqiyyūn*, pp. 139, 145).

4 Interpreting the texts of the eighteenth and nineteenth centuries

The conditions of Baghdad and Baghdadi scholars

In the eighteenth century, Baghdad retained its position as a major city, with multiple markets and a place for Hajj caravans to assemble, in addition to continuously holding the seat of central government. Yet it appears that the honorary position of Baghdad as a major learning centre has weakened in this century. The permanent migration of scholars due to unstable situations enabled scholars to move to the adjoining cities and establish further learning centres. Despite the positive aspect of founding multiple learning centres, the move of scholars outside Baghdad resulted in some negative ramifications, such as interruptions to writings and the loss or damage of some valuable books. However, in the nineteenth century, the general conditions of Baghdad improved, as occasional tragic events such as sieges, fights, floods and epidemics became less frequent. Subsequently, Baghdadi learning centres partially retained their affluence.

A number of eminent scholars and intellectual leaders stayed in Baghdad, though reverse migration inside and outside Baghdad continued. These conditions made it a difficult task to find a scholar who had stayed in Baghdad for a long time. Since the literature of this period is abundant, the focus will be on the work of three scholars. First, the famous poet, shaykh Kazim al-'Uzari; second, the historian and religious scholar shaykh 'abd al-Rahman al-Suwaidi; and finally, the poet and religious scholar shaykh Salih al-Tamimi. Also, texts of other scholars are examined to outline some ideas that are not clearly displayed in the writings of the selected scholars. The writings of these scholars portray specific concepts of the eighteenth and nineteenth centuries, and indicate remarkable observations of Baghdad's architectural and urban development at that time. To understand the circumstances of these scholars, I am including a brief explanation of their lives, in addition to their writing styles.

Shaykh Kazim al-'Uzari

The poet shaykh Kazim al-'Uzari was among the most prominent scholars in eighteenth-century Baghdad. He belonged to a dignified family, which included a number of scholars.[1] In the early seventeenth century, al-'Uzari's family immigrated to a neighbourhood called *ràs al-qurayya* in eastern Baghdad,[2] where he was later born in 1143/1730.[3] The name *'uzari* came from his grandfather who used to sell a particular kind of clothing, called *'uzur*.[4] Like other scholars in the area, al-'Uzari studied Arabic literature, Qur'anic interpretation, Islamic disciplines, history, theology, philosophy and astronomy. He excelled in literature and wrote eloquent poems at the young age of twenty. Shubbar notes, "no one in Baghdad was able to write eloquent poems better than al-'Uzari".[5]

Historians describe al-'Uzari as proficient in debating, quick minded, smart with a powerful memory and full of humour.[6] At one stage, he moved from *al-rusafa* to *al-karkh*, where he spent the rest of his life. He died in *al-karkh* in 1212/1797 and he never returned to his home in *al-rusafa*.[7] Al-'Uzari's poems proved popular in the society of Baghdad, since they combined uniquely fluent language and a pleasant style and were saturated with powerful meanings. They also enclosed sympathy for tragic events that occurred in Baghdad. The reading of al-'Uzari's writings embraces a wealth of genuine ideas about the social atmosphere of the city and its urban landscape, in addition to different architectural forms. These poems are full of sensitivity and delicate emotions, and they include a lot of metaphoric images and complicated notions that require a profound analysis to expose their meanings.

Shaykh 'abd al-Rahman al-Suwaidi

The historian and religious scholar 'abd al-Rahman al-Suwaidi was a famous scholar of Baghdad in the eighteenth century. His family[8] moved to Baghdad from Dur in the late sixteenth century and settled in the western part of the city.[9] Al-Suwaidi was born in 1133/1721 in a neighbourhood called *khidr al-yas* in *al-karkh*. At the age of 11, he moved with his family to Hilla due to a siege on Baghdad in 1145/1732, but they returned to Baghdad shortly afterwards. This temporary move gave him a chance to learn from other prominent scholars and poets in Hilla.[10] Some of these scholars had lived in Baghdad, but they moved for different political and social reasons. At the age of fifteen, al-Suwaidi enrolled in a high school in eastern Baghdad. He started to write poems in his late teens and started teaching in *al-rusafa* schools in his early twenties. This indicates the learning centres in eastern Baghdad were still effective.

In 1156/1743, another siege was enforced on Baghdad, and al-Suwaidi had to move from *al-karkh* to live in fortified *al-rusafa*, where he stayed about a year with his younger brother. Although he left *al-karkh* for a relatively short time, and although he was still living in Baghdad, he missed *al-karkh* very much, and he expressed sad emotions in his poems. While the fortified eastern part comprised important facilities and contained fine buildings, it lacked comfort and freedom. On the other hand, with its natural beauty and calm atmosphere, *al-karkh* evoked more love and attachment. Unlike al-'Uzari who did not have strong relationships with the Mamluk governors, al-Suwaidi's family established good relationships with some of them at certain times.[11] These affairs influenced his writing style; he wrote a number of books and poems to document the life history of these governors.[12] He also wrote other historical books that document various stages of Baghdad's history.[13]

In his book *tārīkh ḥawādith Baghdad wa al-Basra*, al-Suwaidi documented the events of 1772–1778. This book took the shape of a diary of the author's trip from Baghdad to Basra when plague hit Baghdad in 1772, causing a severe loss of lives.[14] Soon after the danger stopped, al-Suwaidi wanted to return to Baghdad, but Omar *pāshā* ordered him to stay in Basra, and work there as a qadi.[15] He was warmly welcomed in Basra, and was appointed as a judge and a teacher. He missed Baghdad dearly, though, and kept attempting to return until he finally reached Baghdad in 1188/1775. Al-Suwaidi expressed his suffering and longing for Baghdad in his writings. He retained his love and admiration for *al-karkh*, though he also expressed appreciation of *al-rusafa*, which suggests some positive change there in the late eighteenth century. He died in *al-karkh* in 1200/1812.[16]

Shaykh Salih al-Tamimi

The poet and religious scholar shaykh Salih al-Tamimi was among the renowned scholars of Baghdad in the early decades of the nineteenth century. Al-Tamimi was born in *al-kazimiyya* northern Baghdad in 1189/1776. He belonged to a knowledgeable family that included many prominent scholars, like his grandfather shaykh 'Ali al-Zayni. At an early age his father died, and he moved with his grandfather to Najaf,[17] and then moved to Hilla where he stayed for a while. Al-Tamimi studied many subjects and attended many scientific debates in Hilla between his grandfather and other scholars, which advanced his knowledge considerably. He started to write eloquent poems in his teens, and he was well-known for his improvised works. He was also recognised for having an easy personality, a sense of humour, a quick memory and plentiful knowledge.[18]

Throughout his stay in Hilla, during the year 1241/1825, the people of Hilla revolted against the last Mamluks' governor, Dawud *pāshā*. Al-Tamimi composed a number of informal yet constructive poems about this event, which amazed everyone and evoked a great deal of appreciation for their fluency and unique style.[19] Consequently, Dawud *pāshā* was very impressed with al-Tamimi's composing abilities, and ordered him to move to Baghdad, and appointed him the head of *dīwān al-'Inshā'* (the composition bureau). Al-Tamimi stayed in eastern Baghdad for twenty years. During his stay in Baghdad, construction schemes were initiated, and many mosques, schools, markets and other public buildings were either renovated or rebuilt. In addition, housing styles became more decorative, with lots of ornamentation and fine architectural details.

Since it was a tradition at that time to document the date of construction in poetry, al-Tamimi composed many poems in relation to the renovation of mosques and other buildings of Baghdad. These poems contain important insights into the architectural and urban development of Baghdad. Al-Tamimi also wrote about the beauty of Baghdad and the Tigris River, in addition to a number of poems that comprise enthusiasm and ethics. These poems consist of important concepts and vital reflective descriptions of the atmosphere of Baghdad in the early nineteenth century. Al-Tamimi died in Baghdad in 1261/1845.[20] This brief account of the lives of the three selected scholars shows many similarities in their conditions. However, the writings of each scholar included different aspects. While al-'Uzari's poems focused on sensitivity and scientific approaches and their relationships with human behaviour, al-Suwaidi's writings focused on historical accounts and longing. On the other hand, al-Tamimi's poems included various architectural depictions. The overall meanings of these varieties is inspirational to this book's inquiry.

The cityscape of Baghdad

The reading of the literature of the eighteenth and nineteenth centuries outlines a number of urban and architectural settings that form the cityscape of Baghdad. The literature of this period specifies the second settlement of Baghdad. During that time, this settlement consisted of two parts: the eastern part or *al-rusafa*, which was bigger and comprised the administrative complex, and the western part or *al-karkh*, which was smaller and less important. The third main part of the city is the Tigris River that runs between these two parts. The name Baghdad in this literature was typically associated with *al-rusafa*, though it was sometimes associated with *al-karkh* only, or it was linked to the whole city at other times. Importantly, the poets focused on the beauty of *al-karkh*, which implies *al-rusafa* was less inspiring.

Historical materials highlight particular public settings of Baghdad in this period, such as schools, mosques and markets. Whereas literature expands these settings to include other components of the city, including public gardens, learning centres, coffee shops, the bridge, river banks and houses that were partially transformed into venues for cultural fora,[21] I will elaborate on these components to understand the overlooked elements in Baghdad's urban history. Since the three themes – spatial, nostalgic and reflective – are interconnected and embedded in texts, I will refer to them as appropriate. The literature of the late eighteenth century mostly expresses nostalgic and spatial themes, while the literature of the early nineteenth century mostly indicates spatial and reflective themes, which indicates a remarkable improvement in the city's conditions.

The two sides of Baghdad

The texts of the eighteenth century encompass many spatial themes. They draw a magnificent image of the region of Baghdad that is different to the conventional picture that refers to the city's appearance being unappealing. For example, in a poem that was composed to praise Sulayman al-Shawi,[22] al-'Uzari highlights the beautiful image of Baghdad in the late eighteenth century:

> If you mention beautiful places in the area
> Do not forget the crescents of *al-zawra* '
> This land overflows with beauty from its sides
> The beauty pours like rain that pours from the sky
> I wonder if this is only a city or is it heaven on earth!
> Or is it a rosy cheek of a beautiful girl!
> I ask you my friends; will the good times ever come back?
> And would the calm shade be delivered again by the grand green tree!
> I salute those wonderful nights from the past
> They were bright and full of dignity and eminence[23]

This poem begins with a description of beauty in all its dimensions. Al-'Uzari designates Baghdad as paradise, which indicates exceptional natural and spiritual beauties that surround both sides of the city. He also refers to nostalgic historical beauty, by calling it *al-zawra* ' and linking it to the thriving round city, which was built in the eighth century. While the round city demonstrated negative aspects in the history of Baghdad, its magical image was perpetuated in peoples' minds, reminding them of a great history. By using metaphoric elements linked to natural beauty, and by expressing sadness in relation to losing loved ones, the poem suggests an unequal span of the measures of beauty at that time.

The image of late-eighteenth-century Baghdad drawn in this poetry suggests a high level of beauty, represented by the natural landscape and famous history. It also indicates certain nostalgic themes of love, longing and attachment, while incorporating courage and dignity, which relate to social beauty. Al-'Uzari ends the poem by expressing a deep sorrow for the loss of good people, which reduced social beauty[24] and impacted the perception of the city. In a poem that praises another leader in Baghdad,[25] al-'Uzari portrays that leader as a moon. He associates the beauty of the moon with a sweet taste and beautiful smell to outline the dignity of that leader:

> This beautiful moon makes the heart confused about its great beauty
> It cures sickness with its sweet taste
> This moon exalted us with the ṣabā [eastern wind]
> And granted us with fresh breeze that arises from its attractive
>   features[26]

The indication of breeze, beautiful weather and magnificent sky scenes defines more spatial qualities of the city. During that time, eastern Baghdad was enclosed by a defensive wall except at the river's edge,[27] where there were mainly mosques and government buildings. The limited exposure of the residents to the river allowed a more metaphorical perception of its environment, and inverted views inward to the court and upward to the sky. The retreat of social beauty in the late eighteenth century, due to a great loss of people, is also indicated in al-Suwaidi's narratives. He mentions the consequences of the plague in 1772, which forced him to leave Baghdad with his family to survive the epidemic. He expresses nostalgic feelings of longing, pain and distress of losing his friends:

> When plague hit Baghdad and Basra areas, and good men became extinct, and authority was taken by people who don't deserve it, and everything was put in the wrong place, all beauties vanished. After living in peace for a long time, we are now drinking stinking water. I feel that previous nights are like clouds that were cleared away, or an illusion that disappeared rapidly. I also feel that those past nights were like dreams, and the beauties were showing in my sleep, or they were like a shadow that expanded then shrank, or an imaginative idea that came and went quickly, or a plant that grew up then it was suddenly cut off. I thought of this life and its unstable situation of good and bad times, and . . . I found out that being attached to it is the starting point of parting with it. I also found out that dissimulating it is hypocrisy; its water is extremely bitter, and its properties and ownerships are abandonments.[28]

Al-Suwaidi utilises the plague incident as a symbol of bad political circumstances, and he associates the beauty of Baghdad with the survival of good people. He states that when righteous people died out, all kinds of beauty disappeared, since the plague left only bad people alive to take control of everything. Besides the permanent loss of sincere people, for him, being away from Baghdad meant losing the beauties of life. Al-Suwaidi describes peaceful times as sweet water, yet this water became 'stinking' after the disasters that took place. He also describes the taste of water as bitter, using this metaphor to refer to the taste of life. The association of the conditions of the city with the purity and contamination of water indicates its great effect on people, as it symbolises life. Although the taste of water did not actually change, al-Suwaidi describes it as impure. This reveals how the alteration of one measure of beauty interacts with people's imagination to invert the truth, and controls their perception of similar things in different ways.

While in Basra, al-Suwaidi wrote many poems about Baghdad. These poems referred to the city as a whole, and did not focus on its two parts. Despite the differences between both parts of the city, when people leave, the two are perceived as a whole. These texts also show that the connections between both parts of Baghdad strengthened towards the end of the eighteenth century. Once again al-Suwaidi associates his love of Baghdad with his loved ones, which confirms the integral effects of social aspects and circumstances on the perception of place:

> For Baghdad I long greatly
> So please 'abu Faraj prepare the she-camels
> And take me there in the dark night without delay or any preparation
> And do not wait for travelling companions
> If the condition is urgent and if someone like me feels greatly irritated
> He will not wait for a companion
> I mentioned my loved ones and my longing increased
> My love reached the highest limit, like the soul that reaches the throat
>   of a dying person[29]

This poem expresses nostalgic meanings of love and longing for Baghdad. It states a great deal of suffering and emotions, which is conveyed through an imaginative trip back to Baghdad. In the last line, al-Suwaidi used the word *fawāq*[30] to express his urgent need to go back to Baghdad, otherwise he will die soon. He borrowed this word from the Qur'an, where it indicates the definite punishment given to the unrighteous after they die, as they have no chance of being brought back to life.[31] The beautiful picture of Baghdad has expanded to the nineteenth century, with more improvement and less distraction, since the nineteenth century witnessed fewer epidemics and more redevelopment projects. The poet Salih al-Tamimi illustrates fantastic spatial and reflective qualities of Baghdad:

> The heavy rain is travelling between the valleys
> And it meanders through low grounds and highlands
> I testify that beauty has no limitations
> Yet I think there is no parallel to the beauty of Baghdad[32]

The image of Baghdad in these lines encompasses components of natural beauty, such as rain and green lands. It also indicates an overall beauty of the city, which suggests the inclusion of all measure of beauty, including architectural and social beauties. In another poem, al-Tamimi reflects on another meaning of Baghdad:

> There is certain sustenance for its seekers on this earth
> This is a promise and a pledge from God
> No one mentioned that a revelation took place in Baghdad
> Yet I acknowledge that the one who stays in this city is a forerunner to
>   eternity[33]

Al-Tamimi wonders about the reasons for Baghdad's beauty; if it is allied with any spiritual factor, such as a revelation. He verifies specific, beautiful characteristics of place are sustenance from God. He declares that no revelation occurred there, yet he admits the one who stays in Baghdad obtains eternity and fame. This poem brings up another measure of beauty, and shows the outstanding beauty of Baghdad that made al-Tamimi wonder about the unseen willpower to sustain all dimensions of beauty in this city. The textual representation carried out in this section suggested 'integral beauty' as one of the ignored urban themes in the historiography of Baghdad. The texts outlined a number of qualities of Baghdad, including infinite beauty, greenery, impressive environment of the river, strong social relationships and an educated society. These qualities evoked great love for and attachment to this land, along with the great appreciation of its beauty.

The representation of al-karkh

The western part of Baghdad (or *al-karkh*) has been overlooked as a remarkable component of Baghdad's urban history. The eastern part (*al-rusafa*) is always highlighted because it was bigger, and it was the hub for successive governments. Besides, it had been surrounded with defensive walls since the Abbasid period. Consequently, *al-rusafa* sector held the name Baghdad for a long time. The western side was also occupied since the Abbasid period,[34] but its population was less than the population of the eastern side, and it did not have defensive walls until the eighteenth century. When the situation in eastern Baghdad became unpleasant in the late eighteenth century, an expansive move outside the eastern sector occurred.

In the late eighteenth century, the region of *al-karkh* had typical Baghdadi neighbourhoods, with more farms and greenery, and few fine buildings. On the other hand, the eastern side had 'the most excellent and moderate architecture'[35] (Figure 4.1). However, many people decided to move to *al-karkh* where there was more freedom and less tension. This indicates that the solitary advantage of excellent architecture is not capable of building strong connections to people, and therefore, cannot be the only representative of place. Thus, affection and attachment to place cannot be achieved unless a 'balance' between all dimensions of beauty is maintained.

Al-Suwaidi, who used to live in *al-karkh*, wrote about its attributes:

When I left *al-karkh* it was full of enjoyment
All people gathered with happiness
Everywhere was illuminated with bright lights
And the flowers and the fragmented trees spread in every direction
The *sabā* sustains life in your soul
Its concealed fragrance is originated from this land
The birds on the trees sing with joy
And tender branches move with the breeze[36]

Figure 4.1 Above, a sketch of *al-rusafa* showing less greenery and more architectural components; below, a sketch of *al-karkh* showing extensive greenery

Source: Jones (1998).

Al-Suwaidi illustrates spatial tributes of *al-karkh*. He relates happiness to natural and social beauties, referring to bright lights, flowers, trees, birds and breeze as part of Baghdad's integral beauty and splendour. This poem, and much of the literature of this period, exclusively signify the loveliness of *al-karkh*, and suggest it as a constant locale of beauty. Conversely, the beauty of the eastern side fluctuated throughout the history of Baghdad, depending on various circumstances. Likewise, al-ʾUzari, who was born in *al-rusafa*, where he also spent his youth, considered *al-karkh* his home:

> I send my tributes to those places that were lively
> We enjoyed living there and the rain was pouring constantly
> It is great to have *al-karkh* as my home and to have affectionate
>   neighbours,
> And to have friends who are pleased if I am pleased and who are hurt
>   if I am hurt[37]

Al-ʾUzari expresses nostalgic feelings, and indicates the great role of social happiness in establishing affection and attachment to a particular site. This shows how integral beauty generates feelings of belonging. Still, he maintains an appreciation of both sides, believing that they constituted one whole unit. Al-Suwaidi also expressed nostalgic feelings about *al-karkh* when he had to move to the fully fortified eastern side during a siege that took place in 1156/1743. He stayed in *jāmiʿ* al-ʿAquli, one of the mosques of eastern Baghdad that are close to the Tigris River. This move caused a lot of suffering for him and his fifteen-year-old brother:

> I woke up one night before dawn and felt longing for *al-karkh* and for
> the dawn prayer within those remains. My ample tears flowed and they
> were about to develop into blood.[38]

This statement shows the great joy al-Suwaidi felt while living in *al-karkh*, where natural beauty, social relations and freedom drew a lovely image of the city, despite architectural conditions that he describes as 'remains'. Having less connection with the society of eastern Baghdad, and comparing the enclosed, dense city that had few open spaces and less freedom with the western part, he felt deep sadness and wept continuously. Al-Suwaidi remembers the call for *fajr* (dawn) prayer as if there was not such a call in the eastern part, showing the happiness he experienced in *al-karkh* made him perceive similar calls differently. He mentions the call for this prayer specifically because the call at dawn signifies peace and tranquillity. He also expresses the hardship of being apart from *al-karkh* in poetry:

> Oh my friend, go to *al-karkh* and stay in its deserted places
> Then ask it how did beautiful people leave it!
> When I lived in *al-karkh* it was full of righteous people
> Groups of friends were gathering in its clubs
> So, what happened? And why did people desolate it?
> And where are the old imprints and the high buildings?
> I miss the whole area of the west river-side
> The eastern side is pleasant but it is not similar to it
> I beg you, my friend to stand there like a flag
> That might bring the two separated parts together,
> And do the same thing I did on the day I left
> When lots of tears were pouring down onto my cheeks[39]

For al-Suwaidi, the two sides are not comparable. He keeps remembering *al-karkh* as the best place whose natural, social and architectural beauty dominated his inner imagination. It is striking how *al-karkh* engaged both al-'Uzari and al-Suwaidi and created deep love and pleasure. This love was tested in the case of separation, and caused great pain for both scholars. However, for al-Suwaidi it was a physical separation from *al-karkh*, and for al-'Uzari it was a social separation. The easy access to both sides of Baghdad reflects the freedom of movement between them, and indicates how the Tigris River acted as a linking element rather than a means of urban segregation. Though with more truthful friends and less traitors around, both al-'Uzari and al-Suwaidi were rather pleased to live in *al-karkh* and consider it home. These writings indicate a decrease in the integral appeal of the eastern side in the late eighteenth century. Yet, in the nineteenth century, the conditions became relatively better, and this was reflected in the texts of that period.

The Tigris River

The urban history of Baghdad was associated with the Tigris River since the establishment of the first settlement around three thousand years ago. Due to its central location, Baghdad has been the cultural mediator between northern and southern Iraq and is at the point where the two great rivers (Euphrates and Tigris) are close to each other. Baghdad's urban morphology indicates a strong connection to the edge of the river, which provides a central artery for its growth and acts as a major collective icon of its historical events. It also offers aesthetics, irrigation, security and transportation, and it secures symbolic characteristics related to place, including sunshine, sunset, and beautiful nights with the moon and stars.[40] However, these qualities are not emphasised in conventional sources, which represent the river as an adversity, due to its recurrent flooding.[41]

The river coexisted with other elements that shaped Baghdad. For example, the first urban settlement emerged as a market village on the Tigris River. Also, the round city could not survive for long because it wasn't built directly on the river. So, new blocks began to grow around the walled quarters towards the river, where people retained proximity to the waterway. Conversely, the outer settlement by the river grew rapidly. The Tigris River has been a source of inspiration for poets throughout Baghdad's history to the extent that almost all scholars cited it in their writings. These texts highlight the river's significance as a source of integral beauty that is 'perfected and complete'.[42] Although the river is represented heavily in poetry, it is not always mentioned directly, as sometimes it illustrates the river's environment and the wonderful atmosphere it established in the region. Besides being a source of glory and purity, the urban literature of Baghdad in the eighteenth and nineteenth centuries illustrates the river as a source of love, happiness and blessings. For instance, in a poem dedicated to congratulate Ahmad al-Shawi on *'Eid* occasion,[43] al-'Uzari indicates the happy atmosphere of the river:

> The land is dancing happily; gratified with its noble and generous
>   inhabitants
> And delighted for its complete richness and countless blessings
> This entire beauty is a result of his determination
> The same way stunning gardens are the products of plentiful rain[44]

In this poem, al-'Uzari refers to the environment of the river indirectly, by using metaphoric clues of rich and fertile land, to commend al-Shawi. The river's space was conceptualised through the space of the sky and through some narrow lanes that lead to the river's shores. The above poem remarks spatial qualities, such as beautiful gardens and heavy rain, in addition to a happy and cheerful land. This perfect natural landscape reflects the river's footprint, and the prosperous environment it creates. Another poem by al-'Uzari assigns additional meaning to the river, by considering it a source of relief and tranquillity. Al-'Uzari recalls positive nostalgic characteristics of Baghdad, in order to overcome some harmful events that had resulted in a great loss of loved ones. He reminds himself of the wonderful neighbourhoods that were full of mild breezes approaching from the river's surface:

> The houses of my loved ones are vacant,
> And the antelopes are scattered in the valley

Oh God I can't forget those lovely places;
With the fragrant breeze that comes from the aromatic trees
I wouldn't be able to control my grief;
Without remembering those beautiful Babylonian eyes
That appeared to us between Euphrates and Tigris
Walking elegantly and calmly[45]

Al-'Uzari refers to the happy and calming atmosphere of Baghdad, which undoubtedly relates to the blessings of the nearby river (Figure 4.2). Yet, the city was happier when both lovely friends and natural beauty were combined. The Tigris River and its breeze are presented as comforting and reassuring elements. Al-'Uzari states even though he lost his friends, their fragrance is sustained in that land. This fragrance joins the soft breeze, and fills the place with comfort. He utilises the timeless relationship between beauty and women, as he remembers lovely Babylonian girls during that hard time. The multi-dimensions of this beauty that associates historical, spiritual and material beauties gave him hope and strength. He combines it with the loveliness of the river to maintain a positive feeling during hard times.

The extensive use of aromatic smell in al-'Uzari's poetry to symbolise honoured souls signifies the complexity of place and the importance of considering these unseen measures in the interpretation process. These concepts that are related to the spiritual qualities of place are usually not adequate as historical evidence in conventional historiography. The Tigris River represents contradictory images of beauty and devastation in history. However, the devastating effects of the river are never mentioned in the poetry of al-'Uzari and others. This suggests that the blessings of the river outweighed its negative impacts. Indeed, the whole collection of al-'Uzari's poems is rich in metaphoric depictions of the river's environment. The criteria of the poems and the eloquence of the Arabic language entail meandering representations, yet the main gestures of the river remain explicit. The various interpretations of the river are also demonstrated in al-Suwaidi's writings. In one of his poems, al-Suwaidi expresses his longing to Baghdad while he was away in Basra:

I remembered *al-khuld* [castle] and the souls that flow there;
And the water that gushes forth everywhere
Can I get a sip from that water to extinguish the fire of adoration
        inside me?
As this water comes from *dijla* the pure[46]

These nostalgic impressions embrace various metaphorical meanings and psychological aspects of the river, including quenching thirst with sweet

Figure 4.2 The river's atmosphere

Source: Stark (1947).

water, acting as a luxury fringe to Baghdad, and representing natural and soulful beauties. Al-Suwaidi mentions *al-Khuld* castle, one of the luxurious castles built on the edge of the river in the Abbasid period. This castle symbolises the river as a lavish fringe of Baghdad and a source of beauty. Although this castle had disappeared by the time of al-Suwaidi, it was turned into a story that was transmitted through generations and perpetuated in people's memories, recapping their positive past. Al-Suwaidi stresses the fact that souls and happy spirits never vanish or disappear, in contrast to material forms that are subject to continuous alteration.

These texts show outstanding features of the Tigris River's environment embedded in literature. The metaphor of drinking sweet water of the river has been extensively outlined in Baghdad's literature throughout history. This suggests the river, its environment and its water have acquired nationalistic connotations and specific nostalgic qualities, which need to be critically examined in the historiographical studies of Baghdad. The urban literature of the nineteenth century continued to express the river as a source of beauty, prosperity, blessing and tranquillity, with more focus on its spatial qualities. The early decades of the nineteenth century witnessed repairing and reopening of some secondary rivers that flow into the Tigris River. For instance, a poem by al-Tamimi portrays the Tigris River as honourable and dignified, while celebrating the reopening of a small river called *nahr ʿisa*:

> I don't know which one to congratulate more in my poem;
> Shall I commend the river itself or its blessed residents?
> This small river was suffering from old age and ignorance,
> And now, it is strutting like a proud youth
> It yearns to meet *dijla*, the pure and dignified river;
> As everyone longs to a sincere and pure beloved[47]

As a temporary resident in Baghdad, al-Tamimi indicates reflective themes of the river. He describes it as a distinguished pure river that makes other rivers strive for the moment of their reunion with it. The poem indicates the pleasure and social happiness of the river's atmosphere, which made it an honourable feature of the city. In a parallel poem, al-Tamimi indicates more reflective and spatial themes of the Tigris River as a virgin, which all rivers desire, and flow quickly to meet up soon:

> This river is longing curiously for the virgin *dijla*
> And it folds up miles of lands to join it[48]

This poem shows the river's interlocking influence on social modes and emotions. It represents the river as a favourable component of the city, which grants honour to other minor streams that join it. These expressions reflect the dignity of the river in the mind of both the residents and visitors alike.

The bridge of Baghdad

One of the significant components of the urban history of Baghdad is the only bridge that existed in the region for centuries. The connection offered by this bridge between the two parts of Baghdad denoted it as a unique component in its urban history. The bridge is briefly presented in conventional historiography, through a description of its substantial components. It consisted of 34 boats tightened together with strong ropes[49] (Figure 4.3).

Figure 4.3 The boat bridge of Baghdad with a coffee shop on its end
Source: al-Warrak (2007).

On the other hand, the analysis of literature and poetry of the eighteenth and nineteenth centuries indicates other qualities of the bridge. It is worth noting that there was another bridge in northern Baghdad at that time. That bridge connected *al-kazimiyya* and *al-'a'zamiyya* districts, but because these areas were autonomous then, the bridge of Baghdad sustained its position as the main link between both sides of Baghdad.

The boat bridge needed constant maintenance often to prevent breakages caused by strong winds or high water level. However, during eventual damages,[50] boats were used to transfer people between the two sides. As with the river, the bridge of Baghdad is not presented directly in al-'Uzari's poetry. Rather, al-'Uzari points to the two parts of Baghdad in his poems as equally blessed, which shows that they were connected in the minds of the residents and witnessed mutually happy times. In a poem that commends a leader in Baghdad, al-'Uzari states a spatial quality of the river:

> You were sent out from the mountains of *tihamah*[51]
> As a great leader who scented the two sides of Baghdad[52]

Al-'Uzari refers to the connective quality of the river. He also refers to a specific quality, being the pleasant smell. In another poem, al-'Uzari explains in addition to the happy and peaceful times the two parts of Baghdad experienced together, they also witnessed devastating conditions as well:

> Oh my friend, if you are unaware of the meaning of death;
> Then stop your mount on the two sides of Baghdad[53]

These poems represent opposing conditions of the two sides of Baghdad, which reflect the unstable situation of the city. They suggest dichotomy as a significant trope to the urban history of Baghdad. They also indicate the two parts of the city are equally important and they both experienced the same destiny. While the river naturally divides the area into two parts, these texts show the power of integration rather than separation. It appears the bridge's function as a mean of connection and integration of the two parts of Baghdad exposed it to occasional damage. Al-Suwaidi narrates an incident that happened during a conflict, which caused burning of parts of the bridge:

> Among the traps that they [opponents] set for us is the intention to blaze the bridge at night. They ordered a group of men to do this secretly, who went in small boats. Their plan was to throw fire on the boats of the bridge so that the bridge would burn up and the bridge path would be disconnected.[54]

This incident indicates spatial qualities of the bridge and shows its central role, which made it a target for damage. Al-Suwaidi states people in *al-karkh* became aware of the attempt to burn the bridge, so they assigned men to guard the bridge all night. However, their opponents in the other side managed to set fire to four boats from the bridge, and consequently many ropes were burnt, and the bridge was wrecked. Al-Suwaidi portrays sad feelings of watching the bridge being burnt, yet proudly he soon attempted to repair it with the rest of his group:

> When we saw the bridge burning, our enthusiasm increased, and we quickly crossed the river and reached the other side with our boats, and we helped our people from the eastern side . . . After a while that day, the bridge was fully repaired and we replaced the burning boats with four large boats from our side.[55]

This statement indicates the great status of the bridge, and the strong love and dedication it stimulated in the hearts of the residents. These nostalgic feelings encouraged people to protect the bridge both physically and spiritually. When the trouble ended, al-Suwaidi expressed his pleasure in maintaining the bridge. This attentive vision of the bridge shows it as a key component and a collective icon in the urban history of Baghdad.

In the late nineteenth century, after the demolition of the walls of Baghdad and the expansion of many neighbourhoods, another bridge was built, to upkeep easy movement due to the limited capacity of the single bridge.[56] The urban literature of the nineteenth century continued to show appreciation for the old bridge and represent its spatial qualities as a connecting figure between the two parts of the city. It also considered the bridge a significant urban landmark that institutes a sense of direction, by defining other urban forms according to their proximity to the bridge. This approach shows the social influence of the bridge, due to its longevity. Al-Tamimi gives an example of the connotation of urban forms with this bridge:

> A *jami'* nearby the *jisr* [bridge] was hit by an army of old age;
> It was forced to be damaged by the sword of long era
> Until Dawud undertook its restoration,
> He got the arrows of time to advance it to glory[57]

This poem underlines the restoration efforts that took place in the early decades of the nineteenth century. The maintenance of heritage mosques contributed to their stability and continuity. Al-Tamimi classifies *jami' al-'asifiyya* as *jami' al-jisr* (the bridge mosque). He relates this mosque to the only bridge of Baghdad, because of its proximity to that bridge. This mosque was originally an old masjid and a madrasa built in 1017/1608, and it was renovated in 1241/1825 during the time of Dawud *pāshā*.[58] It was called *jami ʿ al-mawla khāna* before the renovation, but it was named *jami ʿ al- ʾasifiyya* afterwards. The association of the name of this mosque to the bridge indicates the unique status of the bridge and its major role in Baghdad during that period. The urban literature examined here suggests a different phenomenological approach to writing the history of the city, by recognising other elements that help in comprehending space such as smell, taste, relationships and spirituality. These integral aspects of beauty suggest the Tigris River and the bridge as key components of the urban history of Baghdad. Connection and urban significance are the most spatial and reflective qualities of the bridge, while pride and nationalism represented the nostalgic qualities of the bridge.

Public gardens

In the contemporary context, gardens are understood as autonomous urban features that present both social and visual phenomena. Conventional understanding of gardens in the Ottomans' period limits the meaning of gardens to private gardens that acted as social experiences and public hangouts.[59] This reserved function of gardens restricts the capability of possessing gardens to rich people. This meaning has predominated for a long time. Conversely, the meaning of gardens in the urban literature of Baghdad holds a much broader capacity, since it presents pictures of astonishing gardens that are accessible to all, with metaphoric images that express the whole city as a magnificent garden filled with flowers. In addition to the general meaning that links gardens to visual beauty, urban literature conveys multiple meanings of gardens, relating them to social pleasure, wisdom and knowledge.

In Baghdad, gardens are usually associated with the river, which is the main artery that grants blessing to the lands and brings happiness, alongside aesthetic, security and transportation services. In the eighteenth century, huge areas of eastern Baghdad were not fully developed. These areas contained farms and semi-private orchards. Other urban spaces in the city encompassed various gardens within their boundaries, including waterfront mosques, schools, coffee houses and large houses. The interaction between these spaces and their enclosed gardens provided their own manner of sociability within the larger public space. On the other hand, the western side of Baghdad contained a greater number of orchards and gardens. From there, fruit and vegetables were transported to the eastern side.[60] The relatively lower land and the great number of creeks on the western area explain the intensity of plantation there.

The word 'garden' or its Arabic substitute *ḥadiqa* is not indicated frequently in the urban literature of this period, since this word portrays any land with trees and plants that is surrounded by a wall. Instead, the word *rawḍa* is used heavily in literature to present gardens. This word denotes a beautiful green land that either contains, or lies within, the vicinity of a water source.[61] This term signifies the role of the Tigris River and its subdivisions in the thriving of these lands. Thus, the heavy use of the word *rawḍa* suggests an expanded meaning of gardens that goes beyond limited bounds, to outline a much more open space in the city. Al-'Uzari associates various spatial meanings with the notion of *rawḍa*. In a poem that was written to commend the leader Ahmad al-Shawi for his efforts to solve a conflict in Baghdad, al-'Uzari links the meaning of *rawḍa* to the divine power and to life. He describes al-Shawi as a heavenly garden of goodness that restores bodies and souls:

> You secured Baghdad from every possible disaster
> What great protection Baghdad has gained!
> It was like a caravan that lost its way,
> But after this wander it has got assistance
> You are a divine *rawḍa* of blessings,
> That grants life to souls and bodies[62]

This poem outlines a number of aspects that constitute a perfect garden, including divinity, productivity and liveliness. It also shows the amazing image of gardens that existed in the mind of al-'Uzari, reflecting his satisfaction and appreciation of the attributes of Baghdad. That image has extended to comprise different conditions of life. Another poem by al-'Uzari presents nostalgic themes. It links the concept of hope with gardens, and associates sadness with the search for the 'garden of hope' and its extravagant perfumes:

> Oh sorrow of the heart, where is the *rawḍa* of hope?
> And where can I find its aromatic fragrance!
> The scent of dawn dropped by the horizon of sky
> But our sphere missed the aroma of apples[63]

Al-'Uzari draws a magnificent picture of the garden of hope, which has a variety of aromas. He signifies the olfactory sense as a prevailing element in this garden. This gives the garden its identity, since the diversity of senses dictates the distinctiveness of the fragrance, and its amount. Al-'Uzari connects the aroma of the garden of hope with the characters of his loved ones who have passed away. He claims even though the strong fragrance of those people has disappeared, there are still other fragrances in the air. These aromas do not have the same qualities, but they still scent the air, and give hope to heal his deep emotional wounds. In another poem, al-'Uzari focuses on the issue of sociability and relates the continuity of gardens to the presence of community:

> Your absence made my eyelids pour heavily
> My tears boosted my sickness; similar to rain that normally fertilises
>   lands
> These are the empty houses, so enter them my friends;
> You will realise the unstable situation of gardens and their guests[64]

Al-'Uzari associates the lifetime of gardens with the coexistence of their visitors, as gardens may experience decline if the number of guests decreased. He also asserts that excellent features of gardens are not stable, since they turn on changes in social circumstances. The recurrent use of gardens in the poetry of al-'Uzari to symbolise different situations suggests the presence of many gardens at that time, which affected the poet's feelings and imagination. These texts exemplify the features of gardens to represent the situation of life in general. Al-Suwaidi's writings also contain many depictions of gardens. For instance, in a poem that he wrote while he was away from Baghdad, al-Suwaidi illustrates nostalgic themes, describing his beloved city as a garden that is filled with beautiful flowers all year round:

> My heart would not be burnt with the grief of distance
> Except for you, oh town of *al-zawra'*
> Your soil is irrigated with rain and richness
> And generous clouds granted you honour
> Your land is green in all seasons, not merely in spring
> And your flowers blossom in summer and winter[65]

This poem draws a picture of Baghdad as a stunning garden that is flourishing regularly, signifying the interconnection of all urban forms to produce this unified standard of joy. It also indicates a beautiful image of both sides of Baghdad in the late eighteenth century that is appealing visually, socially and spiritually. Permanent flourishing flowers symbolise continuous liveliness of the natural landscape and social settings, in addition to some stability of architectural items.[66] This vision is also expressed in the texts of the nineteenth century, yet the description of *rawḍa* in this literature is more focused on spatial and reflective themes, with more joyfulness and less sadness, indicating a remarkable change in the situation of the city. Al-Tamimi wrote:

> This is a *rawḍa* that was irrigated by a heavy cloud
> That granted it with a fabric full of red and yellow colours
> Every time the breeze passes by it

It bestows us with musk arousing from a fresh land
I imagine it like the *sundus*[67] of the angel Ridwan[68] in paradise
Because of the mass beauty granted to it by water[69]

Al-Tamimi draws a brilliant picture of the city as a garden that contains many brightly coloured flowers. These spatial qualities are linked to the river as a source of all types of beauty. The poet employs this picture to compare Baghdad to paradise, which suggests an ultimate beauty in all dimensions. Although al-Tamimi illustrates the beauty of both sides of Baghdad in his writing, he more often refers to *al-karkh*, which suggests that, compared to the eastern side, the land on that side remained open and contained larger areas of greenery. The analysis of these writings show that they elaborated the integral beauty of the city and employed the senses of smell and taste to highlight the perceptive aspect of this beauty. Spatial, nostalgic and reflective themes are expressed in these texts through happiness, loveliness and divinity. The texts also outlined extra meanings of gardens, which were not simply confined to a piece of land with a variety of plants, but they were expanded to encompass social and historical perspectives of the city. The city communicated its beauty through the interrelationship of all these elements. The idea of the whole city as a garden asserts comfort and happiness despite frequently changing situations.

The urban settings of Baghdad

The exploration of the cityscape of Baghdad in the eighteenth and nineteenth centuries highlighted *al-karkh*, the Tigris River, the bridge of Baghdad and public gardens as the most influential aspects of Baghdad's cityscape. In this section I will investigate more urban settings in that period and explore their further meanings through literature's interrogation. These settings include learning centres, markets and coffee shops. The significant aspects of the urban settings of Baghdad during that time are flexibility, multi-functionality and complete integration with society. The harmony and similarity of designs of different buildings allowed simple transformation of functions whenever necessary. This flexibility encouraged more interrelationships between people and allowed greater fulfilment of society's needs.

Learning centres

In the eighteenth and nineteenth centuries, learning centres were the most distinctive urban features of Baghdad. These centres were a great place for social activities beyond the function of worship and learning. I refer to complexes that comprise both mosques and schools as 'learning centres' since they were integrated in many ways and share both physical space and function. So, it is beneficial to discuss them together and recognise their interrelationships. The remarkable aspect of these centres was their multi-tasking, as they "were centres not of education, or even learning per se, but of the art and authority of writing".[70] So, the association between writing and space is strongly recognised in these places. In Baghdad, many mosques and schools were built on the edge of the river. The significance of these buildings, the safety of the waterfront location, the proximity to the bridge that offers easy accessibility from both sides of Baghdad, and the availability of water for drinking and purification explain this attention to waterfront locations. A great number of these buildings have survived for a long time, adding to the city's historical significance.

The urban literature of the eighteenth century recognises their learning and teaching roles more than their physical structure. These centres had a great character to the degree that Baghdadi scholars associate their recognition of leaders with their appreciation of knowledge and their support to scholars. For example, al-Suwaidi praises Sulayman al-Kabir as follows: "he loves to deal with scholars to a great extent".[71] The poetry of al-ʾUzari comprises numerous hints about learning and knowledge, in addition to highlighting scientific facts metaphorically:

> Science is a massive and boundless sea
> The one who drinks from it is blessed and never becomes thirsty
> It's your choice to be like the space full of darkness or like the illuminated cores
> The enlightened core is not similar to heavy dusk[72]
> You did not realise that you are an element of noble qualities
> These elements cannot be transformed in any reaction
> You have a wisdom that made life continue
> As the skeleton cannot be alive without the soul[73]

This poem indicates spatial and reflective themes by adjoining scientific and spatial qualities with spiritual qualities. Al-ʾUzari was clever enough to write complex poetry, in which scientific facts are woven and embedded to represent different meanings symbolically. In this case, the verses represent a direct ethical meaning and a covert scientific fact. With the twofold manner he refers to scientific laws to signify the traits of that leader, while he explains them indirectly. This 'spatialisation' of knowledge expresses artistic and imaginative meanings within scientific facts. Among these scientific laws are the law of reason and the law of gravity:

> Tell me about good luck which is expected and undeniable
> Since good luck is a sea that is generated by intentions

Without observing the planets from above
The core of iron and steel would not have gravity[74]

This stanza points out the explicit meaning of ethical principles that tie everything together and control the social systems in life, exactly as gravity controls the movement of the planets. These verses outline the influential relationship between scientific attitudes and humanistic approaches, which complement each other to present a whole unit. This confirms the principles of integrated interpretation that avoids isolating scientific qualities from other qualities. Besides using scientific laws to explain various meaning, al-'Uzari present nostalgic themes in relation to knowledge. He considers learning a great retreat from the difficulties of life:

I believe life is pleasant,
Yet it might become boring when your beloved ones are gone
So, my friend, let's plunder these long hours, by seeking knowledge
    of a high rank
And endeavour to forget past tragedies[75]

Al-'Uzari's great awareness of science shows the variety of subjects that were taught then. The comfort expressed in these poems points out the significance of those learning venues as places of sociability and entertainment, in addition to their teaching roles. Similarly, al-Suwaidi indicates a great pleasure in knowledge and knowledgeable people. For instance, he recognises the knowledge of Sulayman al-Shawi as follows:

He is a scholar who is acquainted with knowledge and a cleric who has a plentiful understanding of different subjects. He has edited many books and composed useful writings.[76]

The appreciation of knowledge is correlated to the appreciation of learning centres, since they constitute the settings for the learning process. Thus, it can be assumed that learning centres were effective even though some of them were partially damaged due to constant floods or troubles. When the plague spread everywhere in Baghdad in 1772, al-Suwaidi escaped secretly with his family; as the *walī* of Baghdad, Omar *pāshā* disliked people leaving the city. al-Suwaidi made his way to Karbala, south of Baghdad, and then moved to Hilla. When the epidemic reached those cities he travelled further south to Basra. He expressed pleasure in visiting Basra, stating he was always keen to visit it, because he knew it had great learning centres and many scholars. When he reached Basra, he was well received by the scholars there, who offered him a spacious house and asked him to present lectures in masjid al-qibla. He wrote:

> I liked their learning scheme, and I enjoyed being with them, and they enjoyed my companionship.[77]

Al-Suwaidi expresses great pleasure in being with these scholars of Basra. These reflective themes are also connected to learning. When the plague reached Basra, al-Suwaidi moved to Kuwait, where he was teaching in a mosque called *jāmi'* ibn Bahr. He states this *jāmi'* was similar to a mosque in Baghdad called *jāmi'* al-Qamariyya,[78] which shows the appreciation of knowledge and the pleasant memory of Baghdad's learning centres which enabled him to perceive these cities equally. When the plague eased in Basra, al-Suwaidi returned to teach in masjid al-qibla. Yet, he found that all the people who used to attend his class had died. He was extremely saddened and refused to stay, but he received an official letter from the *wālī* appointing him as a judge and a teacher in Basra. Al-Suwaidi writes that although the job offer was tempting, he did not want to accept it, but he had no choice.[79] He notes:

> After a few days the path to Baghdad was reopened . . . so I sent the whole family in a ship to Baghdad and I stayed alone. In Basra, no one among the high scholars remained alive after plague, except Sayyid Yasin . . . That is why I was missing Baghdad.[80]

Al-Suwaidi expresses loneliness and sadness after the loss of grand scholars in Basra. Although he was offered a good job in a big city, he did not enjoy it, and his longing for Baghdad increased tremendously. The efficacy of learning centres depended on social aspects more than material aspects. Al-Suwaidi expresses these spatial and nostalgic themes in his narratives:

> Be mindful, oh brother . . . that the residents of Baghdad and Basra used to have the most affluent and prosperous life, and the most settled and comfortable period before the attack of plague.[81]

Al-Suwaidi expresses contentment and links prosperity with the existence of scholars living prior to the plague, which suggests the high degree of respect people had for knowledge and their delight in being with the scholars. Al-Suwaidi elucidates the separation from his family and the loss of honourable scholars in Basra were the reasons behind his yearning for Baghdad. Although the epidemic did not affect the buildings, he expressed deep sadness when he returned to Baghdad and found out about the great loss of scholars. So, his affection for Baghdad was significantly dictated by social relationships and scholarly connections. The understanding of these circumstances is crucial to understanding the urban history of Baghdad in that period. The continuous longing for it and its scholars shows that Baghdad had maintained its position as a centre for learning, despite disasters occurring periodically throughout its history.

The literature of the nineteenth century continues to focus on knowledge, with more appreciation of the material structure of learning centres. While a number of centres were erected, "some existing structures were restored and extended".[82] In addition to the restoration of learning centres, the writings express features of social gathering, friendship, love, knowledge, comfort and happiness. For instance, al-Tamimi wrote about the renovation of *jāmi'* al-'Uzbak in eastern Baghdad. This mosque was built in 1060/1650, and was greatly damaged in the early nineteenth century. In 1242/1826 restoration took place, included rebuilding the *jāmi'* and the attached madrasa, maintaining a corner specified for the poor and homeless, and establishing a water tap device, or *siqāya* that supplies fresh water.[83] Al-Tamimi wrote:

> This is a great house for worship;
> If Mina and Muhassab were close to it
> You would not need to travel long distances to reach The House[84]
> If an overbearing person stood in its courtyard,
> His heart will be submissive out of apprehensions to Allah
> If you visit the city of *al-zawra'* then stop at its gate;
> You will see a mosque that prevents ignorance and negligence[85]

Al-Tamimi shows an appreciation of the new settings of that mosque. He establishes connections between the courtyard and the exterior view of the mosque on one hand, and worship and knowledge on the other hand. These remarks suggest the great damage to the mosques of Baghdad at that time had an impact on the learning process, which required rapid renovation. The amazing picture of the mosque drawn by the poet proves the significance of harmonising both material and spiritual qualities to provide an integral beauty of place. It seems that serious renovation efforts of mosques took place in both sides of Baghdad, which implies a remarkable growth of *al-karkh* in the early nineteenth century. Al-Tamimi points to the redevelopment of another mosque called masjid al-Sif in the western side of Baghdad:

> Go, my friend, to *al-karkh*
> You will notice a masjid there
> It has a variety of branches that are blooming with forgiveness

And write down that this masjid is so honoured;
It was constructed on a foundation made of piety[86]

This poetry combines both spatial and spiritual qualities to provide a complete meaning of the renovated mosque. Al-Tamimi associates various subjects of knowledge with the fruitful branches of trees, and connects a physical part of the building, like the foundation, to piety. These metaphoric images enhance the integral interpretation of these spaces through practical means. These texts express a continuous appreciation for the religious qualities of learning centres and the great contentment they invoke. Among significant traditions that usually accompany the building process of mosques, and other buildings in Baghdad, is the tradition of composing a poem to verify the date of the establishment, or restoration of that building. These poems are usually engraved or painted above the entrance of the mosque by professional calligraphers. This tradition was also accompanied by another custom, engraving the establishment date of the *siqāya* that was often attached to the exterior wall for the public. The *siqāya* presented a unique social service and an iconic source of water, which signifies multiple meanings of purity, cleanliness, comfort and pleasure. The social aspect of establishing the *siqāya* added to the social quality of mosques. The following poem verifies the establishment date of a *siqāya* that was built by Sibghat Allah al-Haydari in *jāmi* al-Khulafa in 1260/1844:

This pond quenches thirst with water;
It establishes harmony among bodies and souls
Sibghat Allah initiated the plentiful flow of this water,
For thirsty people, with good arrangements and wise restoration
If you approach this service with a great thirst,
You will drink this cold fresh water with abundant pleasure[87]

These lines indicate other spatial qualities of mosques, and suggest that water reticulation was a necessary service to the learning centres. In addition to schools and *siqāya*, the mosques comprised other social services, such as khans, libraries and shops established to provide the financial requirements of the mosque by the law of waqf.[88] By incorporating various facilities, these mosques grew into large interrelated complexes that presented a platform for a successful social entity. Furthermore, learning centres were among the venues for frequent cultural fora. These fora had developed in Baghdad from its early stages, but they increased significantly in the nineteenth century. These gatherings were intended to educate, entertain and exchange knowledge between scholars.[89]

Moreover, many mosque complexes contained tombs or burial places of dignified people, which added to their significance. In addition to honouring the dead, these urban forms acted as places for worship and social interactions, which greatly influenced the social life of Baghdad. In the nineteenth century, Baghdadis arranged seasonal or weekly visits to these shrines, and they sometimes organised festivals and celebrations there too.[90] This constant respect for those who had passed away was among the unique features of Baghdad, which is noted throughout history for its great number of religious shrines. The poet al-Rusafi articulates the meaning of this tradition:

> Salute these graves, if you are truly alive
> You are pursuing the noble virtue of honouring them
> The person who does not commemorate the martyrs' graves,
> With a lot of respect, is a dead person
> Because respecting the dead is essential even if they are far away
> What if they were close to us?
> These graves can show us,
> The amount of love that is shown by people who are alive, to their
>   homelands[91]

Al-Rusafi states honouring the dead is a deep ethical matter, performed by people who are caring for others. He states this respect is part of the religious teachings. He also notes that people who honour the dead are those who love their homeland, and therefore, they are really alive, and do not just 'exist'. This poem asserts the strong effects of this issue on learning centres and on the urban history of Baghdad as a whole. The analysis of these texts revealed several features of learning centres that show enormous social, cultural, educational, spiritual and emotional scopes of these urban settings. The interlocking attributes of learning centres increased their interface with people's lives, and contributed to their historical continuity.

Markets

The history of Baghdad is strongly associated with market activities. Because of its geographical location and natural resources, its predominant activity since its beginning has been the marketplace. However, the ancient village of suq Baghdad is mentioned briefly in historical texts, because it didn't have a political role in the history of Baghdad. It started to appear in texts after the destruction of the round city, due to the lack of market activities. Al-Khatib al-Baghdadi (d. 392/1071) cites this village in his historical book on Baghdad:

> There was a village in the site of Baghdad, and that village took the name of Baghdad. Every month, a grand suq [market] was held there,

and the merchants go there from Persia, Ahwaz and from cities everywhere . . . in the year 13/634 al-Muthanna al-Shaybani . . . said: I want to raid suq Baghdad village.[92]

Although the markets grew on both sides of the river, they expanded significantly on the eastern side, which suggests that the ancient village (suq Baghdad) survived until the present day as the catalyst for market activity. The long historical recognition of the eastern part as a suq, the appropriate location and easy approach for merchants from various areas in Asia promoted the continuous flourishing of markets. These markets grew into a vital commercial complex that encompasses numerous specialised markets. This specialisation is considered among the important attributes of the markets of Baghdad and all adjacent cities.

In the eighteenth century, the tendency for similar craftsmanship in the same street became stronger, as it helped to defend monopoly rights and to regulate price and quality. These markets comprised shops that followed each other through a labyrinth of arcades, interspersed with mosques and tombs. This practice also "tended to strengthen their other social ties".[93] The name of each market was normally linked to the kind of goods that were manufactured or sold there. For instance, Abadah points out to a specialised market that was built in 1772:

It is at a corner situated in suq *al-jadīd* [new] neighbourhood, and this suq is also called suq *al-laban*. It was called suq *al-jadīd* because it was constructed recently, and was called suq *al-laban* because yoghurt is the main food that is sold there.[94]

The specialised markets were built on the same location of markets since the Abbasid period, when suq Baghdad developed into a big market complex. Examples of these markets are suq *al-bazzāzīn* (drapers' market), suq *al-warrāqīn* (book sellers' market) and suq *al-khayyātīn* (tailors' market). In some of these markets, goods were manufactured and sold in the same location, which increased efficiency and decreased labour and complexities of transportation.[95] These linear markets were effective venues for gathering and socialising. They contained many mosques, in addition to public squares, or *maydāns*, and coffee shops, which made them a significant social component in the city. In addition to trade and social activities, these markets occasionally took on political roles, with gatherings and decorations being prepared for special occasions.[96] Another facility that is usually associated with markets is the khan or guesthouse, which was usually built of two storeys. While the upper storey was occupied with visitors, the lower storey was designed to hold workshops, storerooms and other retail shops.[97]

In the urban literature of the eighteenth and nineteenth centuries, the markets are illustrated infrequently. In contrast to the huge amount of writings about the beauty of Baghdad, the river's environment and learning centres, markets did not attain a similar focus in literature. This suggests that although market activity has been fundamental to the place, Baghdad's prevailing identity at that time as a learning centre and as a beautiful place surpassed market meanings. However, the texts of the eighteenth and nineteenth centuries contain some descriptions of markets. The metaphors of trading activities are embedded in these texts. For example, al-'Uzari uses symbolic meaning of trade to articulate high ethics and nobility:

> I congratulate you Karbala for the beautiful costume you obtained
> Yet this dress is prepared with *yumn* [blessing] and wasn't manufactured in Yemen
> Who can tell the market of that day about this tragedy?
> When the sacred jewels were sold cheaply[98]

Al-'Uzari compares the costume honouring the martyrs in Karbala[99] with a high-quality outfit that is usually imported from Yemen. He utilises the resemblance of the Arabic words *yumn* and Yemen to explain the standing of Karbala in relation to the reputation of Yemeni goods. This indicates active trade between Baghdad and Yemen and the richness of Baghdad's markets in the eighteenth century. In another poem that expresses nostalgic themes,[100] al-'Uzari refers to the goods of Egypt and Persia, which shows vital economic exchange:

> I remember those memorable places that were adorned with costumes
>   from Egypt,
> And they were also decorated with paintings and portraits from Persia
> Though they know my real value, they sold me cheaply;
> As love includes a degree of critique that might underestimate lovers[101]

Al-'Uzari points out the lovely neighbourhoods in eastern Baghdad, which brought him joy during his youth. He depicts pleasant places that are adorned with goods from Egypt and Persia. The poem refers to the effects of migration from the surrounding area to Baghdad before the mid-eighteenth century, which resulted in productive transmission of crafts, illustrative arts and architecture to Baghdad. Usually, memorialising strengthens associations with the past and shows variations in different conditions. Thus, remembering familiar spaces in this poem designates their apparent change and suggests that the commercial activity in Baghdad was more prosperous by the mid-eighteenth century, during the poet's youth. Al-Suwaidi relates the decrease in commercial activities in Baghdad in the late eighteenth century to political problems. He elucidates a clash that took place in 1777 on the position of the governor of Baghdad. He pictures the market at this time as a locale for tension and anxiety instead of relief and prosperity:

> At some of those previous nights, one of the guards of the markets observed some shopkeepers opening their shops at night. Those shopkeepers took away their money from their shops . . . In the morning, the *maydān* was full as usual, and the shopkeepers were busy with their business, as if no one has recognised what happened the night before.[102]

Al-Suwaidi portrays the market's situation that night as full of tension, when soldiers were assembling and preparing for a probable fight. The political situation affected the market and the retail activity to an extent and made the merchants anxious about their belongings, though they strived to act normally the next morning, and the markets maintained their efficiency. These statements show spatial assets of the markets and portray them as lively and active, yet they were exposed to political tensions which made their situation occasionally unstable. It appears that this tension increased a year later, to such a degree that many merchants chose to depart from Baghdad. While he narrates a story about a man who was part of a political conflict in Baghdad, al-Suwaidi relates the decrease in trade in the late eighteenth century to the departure of merchants from Baghdad due to political circumstances:

> That man established good relations with ʿUmar *pāshā*[103] and helped him to oppress people, and encouraged him to take money by force, which made the merchants quit Baghdad and travel far away . . . He also established good relations with ʿabd Allah *pāshā*. When he was appointed as a treasurer, all merchants of Baghdad escaped with their families and their possessions, and the merchants from the borders of Baghdad refrained from entering the city.[104]

This statement shows the consequences of the incorrect decisions of governors on the situation of Baghdad. It also designates more spatial qualities of the markets of Baghdad, showing that they were flourishing before 1778. The merchants had a leading position in the city, and their escape had remarkable effects on society. The reading of these texts highlighted the unstable conditions of the markets of Baghdad in the late eighteenth century. In the nineteenth century, the conditions of the markets seemed to have been improved, as historical narrations show more specialised markets were newly created or rebuilt. In the urban literature of this period, markets were linked to mosques' complexes. This implies the dominant characteristics of the mosques, which granted the markets more recognition and honour by being associated with them. Besides, markets were associated with khans in literature, which entitles dependence as the main features of the markets in that period. Al-Tamimi wrote a poem describing the suq of khan al-Sif, where various grains were sold and stored:

> I swear in the name of Allah;
> He who adorned the sky with special stars
> The person who constructed this building [khan al-Sif]
> Has great determination that could reach the orbits
> I advise the person who is eager to gain profit;
> From all kinds of people, the talking and the mute
> You have to be fair when you measure the goods,
> And never attempt at decreasing weights[105]

Al-Tamimi highlights spatial and reflective themes in these lines. He expresses admiration for a new market complex that was established during the rule of Dawud *pāshā*, but at the same time he conveys his concerns about dishonest retail procedures. The newly developed markets could not be fully effective unless high ethics were combined with physical qualities, to imply that fairness and honesty should be experienced in trade. The representation of Baghdad's markets shows an increasing interest in rebuilding these spaces along with other public settings. Shops were sometimes built to support the mosques financially, or sometimes totally built by individuals. The continuation of specialised markets in this period indicates the perpetuation of these activities in the city. Additionally, the interlocking connections between the mosques, markets and khans resulted in a vibrant complex that delivered a great social experience.

Coffee shops

In the eighteenth and nineteenth centuries, coffee shops were the main places for entertainment and leisure, in addition to gardens. They were major landmarks that were usually situated in strategic locations. During this period, the number of coffee shops increased, and they became an integral part of public spaces and "a commonplace of new waqf establishments".[106] Many of these facilities were attached to mosques, to assist their financial costs. Apart from entertainment, these places increasingly developed into social, cultural and political fora, as they were visited frequently by many scholars and poets, in addition to merchants and other groups. Some historical references suggest the first coffee shop, or what is called *maqhā* in Arabic, was established in khan Jighal by 995/1586.[107] Others suggest that coffee shops had existed in Baghdad since late Abbasid era. They propose that the *maqhā* of suq *al-khaffafin* has specific architectural features similar to *al-madrasa al-mustansiriyya* which was built in the thirteenth century,[108] and therefore it can be assumed that it was built in the same period. Al-Rumaythi suggests this *maqhā* is three hundred years old, which means it was built in approximately the early eighteenth century.[109] Yet there is no evidence that it adopted the function of a *maqhā* then, since coffee was introduced by the sixteenth century, and it might have been renovated or rebuilt in the eighteenth century.

The coffee shops of Baghdad usually serve lemon juice, dried flower tea, dried lemon tea, tea and coffee.[110] Perhaps the name of these shops was associated with coffee because of its connection to the Arab culture. In the eighteenth and nineteenth centuries, the social and educational value of coffee shops increased enormously, as they became a common setting for cultural fora. The increase in writing and the development of printing presses boosted the educational role of coffee shops. With the expansion of Baghdad and population growth, these public places became unique social settings.[111] The urban literature of Baghdad in the late eighteenth century indicates connections to coffee shops. Al-'Uzari advocates coffee over wine, and describes coffee as youthful compared to that elderly drink:[112]

> Black coffee is the best, so enjoy the youth that is embedded in it;
> And avoid that aged item [with white hair] since it's dying soon from
>   old age
> The white part of the eye shows darkness;
> And the black part of the eye proves brightness[113]

This poem confirms the relatively new function of drinking coffee in public places and verifies the growing interest in attending the coffee shops. It is worthy of note that the Arabic word *qahwa* that corresponds to coffee means liquor in Arabic, which implies that coffee took the name *qahwa* because it is infused and has relatively similar effects on appetite.[114] Al-'Uzari uses scientific facts to clarify the features of contrasting colours. The use of colours to interpret ideas in poetry is a powerful method of expression. On one hand, colours appear to be easy to understand, and on the other hand they have eloquent, deep meanings embedded in them. In this poem, al-'Uzari places the interpretation of colours against their common visual meanings as a great philosophy in life.[115] Al-Suwaidi also brings up insights into the conditions of the coffee shops in the late eighteenth century. While narrating the burning of the bridge of Baghdad, he mentions a special coffee market:

> They plundered the khans of grocery that are located in the coffee grinders' market, and they took everything including *tutun* [tobacco for the hookah], gall oak, and soap.[116]

Al-Suwaidi indicates spatial features referring to a specific market, where coffee beans were crushed and prepared for sale in the same place. Although other goods were stored and sold in that market, the name of the market was associated with coffee because it was a dominant product in it. This shows the scale of coffee consumption had risen to a degree that it started to carry a specialised market name. In addition, al-Suwaidi remarks coffee as part of the hospitality of Baghdadis:

> We arranged the supply of bonfires, coffee and tobacco each night, and we provided them with food, days and nights from our side for four days.[117]

Al-Suwaidi shows the generosity of his group during a problem between people from the two sides of Baghdad. He included coffee with food and other supplies, which they prepared for their friends. This statement suggests coffee took on a uniquely luxurious character in the late eighteenth century. Apart from luxury and entertainment, al-Suwaidi refers to coffee shops mostly as meeting places and as notable components of the city:

> They came to the *maydān* and they noticed that the coffee shop that lies on the gate of qal'a [castle] was overcrowding with men and weapons, and they saw the same near the gate of Imam 'A'dham, then they went to the neighbourhood of Muhammad al-Fadl and they found same thing.[118]

Al-Suwaidi designates a number of coffee shops in this narration, which shows the success of these spaces as social settings. These places acted as cultural and political hubs in the city. During conflicts, they turn into hubs for soldiers' assembly. Temporary interferences influenced the conditions of markets, yet they could not affect the continuity of retail and social activities. The increasing number of coffee shops on the river's banks, and the pleasure reflected frequently in texts, attest that their social and entertainment function overshadowed their political roles. In the nineteenth century, the number of coffee shops continued to increase, along with the mosques that were either renovated or rebuilt. Historians cited many coffee shops in their books. Examples of these coffee shops are *qahwat*[119] *hammām al-malih*, *qahwat al-maydan* and *qahwat Na'ila khatun*.[120] A number of coffee shops were also attached to khans and linear markets, but remained parts of the big complex. Some of them were indoor and others were outdoor, depending on their location.

In the poetry of al-Tamimi, coffee shops are not frequently mentioned, as they were considered parts of the mosques' complexes. Yet, indirect hints of coffee shops are embedded in texts. For instance, al-Tamimi wrote a poem

about opening a road and a gate beside the bridge of Baghdad next *to jami '
al-'asifiyya*. This poem reflects spatial qualities of coffee shops indirectly:

> The imprints of Dawud endowed Baghdad;
> With a beautiful costume that brings pleasure to the eye
> *Al-rusafa* was complaining of narrow roads before,
> And everyone hated the tightness
> It was provided with a wide road that decreased congestion, with a
> gate on the bridge
> Surely he who gave these presents to Baghdad is victorious[121]

The gate described in this poem was called *bāb al-jisr*. There was a coffee
shop attached to this gate, located at the end of the bridge (see Figure 4.3). This
coffee shop was mentioned in historical books and was illustrated in traveller's drawings of Baghdad. Because this coffee shop is related to the mosque's
complex and to the nearby bridge, it wasn't highlighted distinctly in literature.

Domes

Although social and spiritual measures had more significance in the scholar's visions of this period, specific architectural elements, such as domes,
are outlined in these texts as identifiers of the unique urban character of
Baghdad. Domes are usually associated with the image of the whole city,
and they are linked to other measures of beauty, including social, material and spiritual qualities. For example, al-'Uzari pictures Baghdad as one
home that constitutes many inviting domes. He considers domes the main
elements that give identity to his homeland:

> Oh home of my beloved, I wish that your domes stay close to a young
> man
> Who is suffering from distance that prevented every hope he had[122]

Al-'Uzari indicates nostalgic thoughts in connection with domes. He associates the familiarity of these forms with hope and comfort, in addition
to friendship and love. This association signifies the symbolic meaning
of domes that makes a place comfortable, embracing and safe. In another
poem, al-'Uzari depicts the quarters of dearly loved people as places of
shelter and refuge. He relates sadness and worthlessness of place to the
destruction of domes and designates the integral role of domes in Baghdadi
society in the late eighteenth century:

> Is there a place similar to those caring clubs?
> They guard the guest and quench his thirst!

My beloved ones promised to leave at night, and they kept their
   promises
What a terrible fulfilment of that painful promise!
Al-ʾudhayb [River] that has never been abandoned, is now deserted
The demolition of those domes forced my loved ones to leave that
   valley[123]

Al-ʾUzari expresses deep sorrow towards losing lovely and brave people
after the plague. The description of neighbourhoods as clubs of protection
and locations of gentle breeze is among the remarkable spatial and nostalgic
pictures of Baghdad drawn by al-ʾUzari. The poem relates to the cluster of
houses as effectively one entity. This unified vision that views architectural
components collectively shows the importance of interlocking all aspects of
the urban experience to attain a complete understanding of that experience.
In a third poem, al-ʾUzari utilises spatial meanings of domes, such as high-
ness, compassion, visual appeal, reception and protection, to identify noble
and dignified people:

I sacrifice my father for the sake of these crescents in the domes[124]
With their brightness, they decorated these roofs with a circuit made
   of turquoise
I say to the land where they were remembered;
The fragrant breeze carries their scent, so enjoy this aroma[125]

Al-ʾUzari notes lovely people would embellish the domes and bless the
land below them with their fragrance. Those people had gone forever, but
their refreshing fragrance persisted. He relates visual beauty and aromas
to knowledge and dignity rather than to material elements. These various
illustrations of domes show the great capacity of architecture to intercon-
nect with other elements and heighten affection and attachment to place.
Further, al-Suwaidi provides other spatial meaning of domes. The beautiful
image of Baghdad that occupied his imagination for long, especially when
he was away from it, completely changed when he went back. He expresses
the sorrow he felt when he returned to Baghdad after a plague struck, which
had killed many good people. He asserts the beauty that he had perceived in
Baghdad was gone. He borrows the idea of the dome to describe tranquillity
in life and express nostalgic notions, yet he accuses life for the sad things he
had experienced and advises people never to trust it:

I am convinced that the one who is deceived by it [life] is in danger, so
   is the one who is attached to it and keeps holding its ropes, which are
   similar to spider threads or weaker. I think whoever seeks refuge in this

life's domes, he resembles the one who is kissing a lion, because he has lost his brain completely.[126]

The domes are not represented as mere architectural forms, rather they are shown as embodiments of life. Usually domes symbolise sanctuary and peace, yet in this statement al-Suwaidi employs symbolism of domes to represent the illusory image of life. This interpretation reflects the multiple meanings of domes. In the nineteenth century, similar meanings were conveyed to those of the late-eighteenth-century texts. However, due to the decrease in epidemics, which lowered death rates, the representation of domes in this century was associated with more spatial and reflective expressions such as loftiness and prestige, rather than longing and remembrance. The following poem describes *jami' al-haydarkhana* in Baghdad:

This mosque is among the houses of Allah that were raised high;
For the worshippers to perform glorification and gratitude
The building was founded on the basis of piety and honesty
He who built it is knowledgeable, patient, fair and generous[127]

This mosque has a large, high dome that was built above the prayer area, accompanied by two smaller domes (Figure 4.4). The poet ultimately indicates spatial qualities of the domes by referring to vast and high spaces

Figure 4.4 Jami' al-haydarkhana
Source: Coke (1927).

created by them. The interpretation of domes in these texts goes beyond the limits of the physical form, since the meaning is interconnected with other social attributes that made the domes dynamic. The interpretation of domes expands to embrace them as a means of interaction between people and as symbols of high standards, facility and loveliness. In regards to the thematic approach, spatial and nostalgic themes are more represented in the literature of the eighteenth century, while spatial and reflective themes are denoted more so in nineteenth-century writings. The multiple meaning of domes in literature adds to the conventional understanding of these forms, which relates them to architectural elements and visual arts, in addition to symbolic divine meanings and spiritual function.

The qualities of houses

The understanding of the houses of Baghdad, and other cities in the region in the eighteenth and nineteenth centuries, is usually limited to domestic meanings. Historical investigation is usually dominated by the study of architectural styles. It observes old houses as part of traditional inquiry that links them to the past, and thus it overlooks their roles in society. The analysis of urban literature intends to explore unexplained features of these houses. These features embrace material structure that is interconnected with natural and environmental modules, in addition to spiritual and social functions, such as cultural fora that were held in the houses of prominent people. There are hardly any clues about the conditions of houses in the eighteenth century, compared to the plentiful studies on the houses of the nineteenth century. The survival of some houses from the nineteenth century into the twentieth century made it possible to examine them thoroughly. Conversely, the loss of historical documents and the great alteration of houses from the eighteenth century explains their limited historical evidence. The texts of this period present houses in relation to the people who lived in them. This ultimate connection opens up a wide range of meanings:

> I recall a house in *dhi al-'araka*
> That is filled with pleasure
> It has fountains that are overflowing with water
> And the great tree makes shadows that dance beneath it
> The guest is protected and the neighbour is safe
> This house offers relief even for the enemies[128]

Al-'Uzari draws a stunning picture of a house that shows all kinds of beauty. In addition to architectural elements like ornamentations and fountains, natural attributes such as water and trees perfected the scene, along with kindness, contentment and protection. Although the poem emphasises several facets of beauty, the water feature was the primary factor of appreciation. The link to water is related to purity, satisfaction and cleanliness. In addition, water represents life in every dimension, since every living feature is made of water.[129] This attitude is inspired by the Qur'an, which includes numerous verses regarding the blissful and happy atmosphere in paradise, associated initially with water. Al-'Uzari mentions the shadows of trees as an additional element that provides comfort and protection. He also implies that safety is not confined to the residents, as the house offers protection to its neighbours and even to enemies if they asked for it. This measure suggests that grouped houses, occupied by people who share similar interests, constituted a successful housing experience in Baghdad. In another poem to grieve for 'abd Allah al-Fakhri, al-'Uzari recalls other spatial and nostalgic qualities of houses:

> I honour those houses that are abandoned now
> They have been places of happiness and generosity
> Their *rawda* and shade are similar to paradise
> The only difference is they are not houses of eternity[130]

This poem illustrates al-Fakhri's house as a reflection of the people who occupied it. The poet places greater emphasis on the social characteristics of these houses. The more benefit they offer to the public, the more the houses are recognised and appreciated. The amount of goodness and generosity presented in these houses, in addition to water gardens (*rawda*) and their shade, makes them parallel to paradise. These expressions show the great influence of religious teachings on the poetry of that period. Al-'Uzari mentions the houses' attributes in a memorialising manner, which suggests some diminution in their qualities by the late eighteenth century. In another poem, al-'Uzari shows passion for the houses of loved ones. He uses 'gentle breeze' in a metaphoric meaning to represent the scent of these places. Although natural air currents are normally associated with the river and other natural elements, al-'Uzari's points out the smell of place was a mix of natural breeze and lively aroma:

> Oh the house of my permanent love;
> I pray that you have everlasting rain and blessings
> Gentle breezes are strolling unhurriedly inside you,
> Like a prisoner who walks slowly with heavy chains[131]

Like many of al-'Uzari's works, this poem expresses spatial and nostalgic themes. It shows the blessings of that house and the specific aroma of his beloved ones. It also indicates the courtyard of houses indirectly, by mentioning heavy rain and breeze that strolls happily inside. Because housing styles of Baghdad in that period constituted attached buildings, the only open space was the courtyard. Al-'Uzari's poetry contains numerous depictions that outline his strong connection to the courtyard space and reflect the inspirational influence of the link to the sky on life inside the house. Al-'Uzari cites his contemplation at night through the courtyard space:

> One night I was awake along with the night star,
> Until both of us turned sore eyed
> Oh the breeze of the valley, where did my friends reside?
> For their sake, tell me truthful news about them[132]

This poem illustrates the courtyard as a means of connection to the sky to seek relief from sadness and grief. Al-'Uzari interacts with the stars and the wind, and he relates his dialogue with them to express his feelings. The interaction with the breeze establishes a horizontal connection, while involving the stars adds a vertical connection, yet both bonds prove the benefit of the courtyard space that provided that direct, multidimensional link. This poem gives further meanings of stars, including nobility, hope, brightness and resilience. In another poem that also shows nostalgic expressions, al-'Uzari narrates the planets and the moon during a period of sadness:

> Who can help me get those moving planets to come back?
> They are praiseworthy in their initial appearance and in their return
> The moon at night always reminds me of my beloved moons,
> As things are always associated with their matches[133]

Al-'Uzari likens his friends, who had passed away, to the moving planets to explain their changing condition. Their beauty and brightness would enlighten the darkness whether they stayed or moved away. This specifies strong social bonds between scholars and the great appreciation of nobility and high ethics in the society. The extensive use of elements of the sky in these texts indicates that the poet spent long hours reflecting at night, interacting with the sky, and praying to God. These texts show the comforting effects of raising the eyes to the sky in the case of sadness and grief, which reveals a continuous religious awareness in the mind of the poet. This signifies an additional connecting role of the open courtyard in houses, apart from lighting and ventilation. Due to lack of accessibility through the city lanes to the river's shores, open courtyards established links with the sky space to compensate for the river's absence.[134] These remarks suggest multiple roles for the courtyards, both physical and spiritual. Al-Suwaidi also expresses spatial and nostalgic qualities of the houses of Baghdad. He describes them as fine big houses, and he considers his home as a place of sanctuary and peace:

> When I moved back from Basra to Baghdad, I wanted to escape from the foreigners, and I was keen to meet my friends and my loved ones. I saw that the plague exterminated my nearest and dearest and all good people and left evil people alive . . . So, I decided to stay away from this corruption, and I chose to hang about alone at home, and occupied myself with my books.[135]

Al-Suwaidi explains the situation of Baghdad after the plague hit in 1772. He had to leave Baghdad, so he went to Basra to escape the epidemic. He suffered greatly during that time, and when he returned to Baghdad in 1775 he discovered the death of many Baghdadi scholars. This loss provoked deep sadness and changed his views of the city dramatically. Al-Suwaidi blames disease for the great loss of good people and the increase in bad people, showing the symbolic meaning of the epidemic that represents social attributes of the city dominating other attributes. During a clash in 1777 on the position of the governor of Baghdad, al-Suwaidi decided not to support either group of opponents. He states, "I believe Islamic law and logic imply that we do not support anyone, as Baghdad's rule would not become possible for everyone but for a great leader".[136] So he stayed at home for a while, but later decided to participate in the conflict. The house in this case was a peaceful place that offered comfort and relief for him. He wrote:

> I haven't experienced the pleasure of safety
> Until I stayed at home and became a close companion to my books[137]

Al-Suwaidi designated his home as his sanctuary during that hardship. He associates it with reading and writing, which reveals another feature of these houses that usually contained special study rooms. These texts express multiple functions of houses. While they represented a high standard of privacy and its interrelated issues of comfort and safety, they also represented significant social meanings. Nevertheless, the literature of the nineteenth century reveals more architectural descriptions of houses. Al-'Alusi narrates that all houses in the nineteenth century contained open courtyards that allowed movement of light and air to reduce excessive heat.[138] He notes that many houses were built with two storeys, and that before that time, the houses were built with one storey, and their exterior walls were not very high.[139] He also states that the houses of rich people were bigger and had more ornamentations than other houses.[140] Al-'Alusi further identifies some luxurious houses that were built in the early nineteenth century, like the house of his grandfather. According to these remarks, it can be assumed that most houses in the eighteenth century were built with one storey. Yet in the nineteenth century, two-storey houses increased gradually, until they became the dominant style towards the end of that century. The poet ʿabd al-Baqi al-ʿUmari[141] wrote a poem describing the house of al-ʾAlusi's grandfather:

> The porch of Shihab al-din is vaulted with honour and glory,
> It is celebrated with knowledge and recognised with grace
> There are many rooms of contemplation in this house,
> As if the blessings of generous river of Talut are accessible
> The most beautiful stars are jealous of this place,
> As every noble man in the universe is subjected to envy[142]

Al-ʿUmari illustrates the great features of this house and shows the luxurious aspects of its design. He commends utilisation of the place for the purpose of knowledge and agrees that it adds more beauty to it. This house was built in the late eighteenth century and was renovated and extended in 1252/1836. Al-ʿUmari outlines outstanding architectural qualities, which reflects a remarkable progress in conditions of Baghdad in the nineteenth century. The poem also indicates the social and educational efficiency of these houses and the easy access they provide for the public. These remarks interlock all dimensions of beauty, including social and learning beauty, and generate an effective approach to housing. Another example of the houses that were built in that period is the house of Muhammad Saʿid al-Mufti. Al-ʾAlusi describes it in the following statement:

> It is a fine house that has amazing architectural features. It was skilfully built, and it has a spacious courtyard. He [al-Mufti] built a fascinating room inside this house, similar to the rooms in paradise, because its walls and roof are beautifully decorated.[143]

This statement reinforces high-status housing styles, and reflects the advancement in architectural techniques and materials to a degree that the space becomes comparable with paradise. This house was a venue for cultural fora for a long time. The extensive ornamentation in some rooms of the house indicates the importance of public learning and social relations. These rooms were heavily decorated, since they were used as formal guest rooms and as learning places. They were also well oriented in the upper floors of big houses, in order to control the amount of sunlight and winds. The quoting of Talut River that is cited in the Qurʾan and the association of the rooms to paradise suggest the continuous influence of Qurʾanic analogies on the literature of the nineteenth century. Al-'Umari also wrote about the same house, asserting that its attractive features inspired scholars to write about it:

This house was built by Sa'id, who is contented in both this life and the hereafter[144]
He had excellent vision that gave the house exceptional features
The one who resides in this house and the one who visits it are the happiest
It provides safety for all people and prevents disasters
By God I swear, this house is a sanctuary for excellence;
I wonder how many secrets are in this house that lurk in its corners[145]

This poem indicates spatial qualities that are interlocked with spiritual qualities. It draws an inclusive image of the characteristics of houses that provide such a pleasant atmosphere. The overall meaning of the house is the product of the interrelationship between all its features. These influential elements include spiritual inspiration, sophisticated vision and social pleasure, expressed through other values such as generosity, kindness, safety and protection, in addition to knowledge and learning. In another poem, al-'Umari expresses his appreciation of his own house in eastern Baghdad:

Is this a gorgeous doll in a castle or is it a bride?
That has a necklace made of stars from Gemini
When it appeared it manifested itself and beautified *al-zawra'*
With its attractiveness and ornamentations[146]

The above lines are among the few lines that portray houses from outside, in contrast to other poems that reflect their outstanding features from within. Because houses were attached to each other and overlooked relatively narrow streets, the exterior of the house offered fewer interesting qualities than its interior. However, it seems that the progression in architectural techniques expanded to include both the interior and exterior of houses. Likening bright objects to jewellery and stars indicates the prosperity and loveliness of the place. Also the bride and the castle symbolise notable architectural development that reminded al-'Umari of historical notions of wealthy kingdoms. Ultimately, the poet associates pleasant impressions with the overall image of Baghdad, which reveals the improvement in visual beauty as well. Although it is obvious that houses that reached these high standards belonged to rich and well-known people, these measures gradually expanded to a wider range of houses. These texts reflected a considerable advancement of houses in the nineteenth century. They revealed additional meanings of the houses of Baghdad, and they highlighted a number of elements that add to the understanding of place, such as conversation, scent and imagination. In comparison to the houses of the eighteenth century, literature presented their social and spiritual qualities, with fewer expressions of material qualities. However, nostalgic and spatial expressions added additional meanings to those houses.

Notes

1 Among the scholars of al-ʾUzari's family are shaykh Muhammad Rida, shaykh Yusuf and shaykh Masʿud.
2 Shubbar, ʾadab al-ṭaff, p. 30.
3 According to Abadah, ràs al-qurayya neighbourhood lies in the same place as the Abbasids' administrative centre (dār al-khilāfa) close to suq al-warrāqin (book market). See Ràuf, al-ʾiqd al-lāmiʿ, p. 317.
4 Shubbar, ʾadab al-ṭaff, p. 29.
5 Al-ʾUzari was highly knowledgeable in tafsīr (Qurʾanic interpretation), hadith (the Prophetic traditions), theology, Arabic philology and historical sciences. See Shubbar, ʾadab al-ṭaff, p. 29.
6 Shukur, diwān al-ʾUzari al-Kabīr, p. 19.
7 Al-ʾUzari was buried in al-Kazimiyya district of northern Baghdad. See Shukur, diwān al-ʾUzari al-Kabīr, p. 27.
8 Al-Suwaidi's father, ʿabd-Allah al-Suwaidi, was also a religious scholar, who taught in al-madrasa al-marjāniyya, and composed many books. See Ràuf, al-ʾiqd al-lāmiʿ, p. 369.
9 Ràuf, tārīkh hawādith Baghdad wal-Basrah, p. 16.
10 At this stage, al-Suwaidi received his first certificate from the Sufi shaykh Muhammad bin ʿAqila al-Hanafi al-Makki (d. 1149/1737). See Ràuf, tārīkh al-ʾusar al-ʿilmiyya fi Baghdad, p. 179.
11 Al-Suwaidi's father, ʿabd-Allah, established strong relationships with the wālī Ahmad pāshā who had ruled Baghdad since 1136/1732. Consequently, Ahmed pāshā appointed him as a mufti of both Karbala and Najaf territories, and assigned him an annual salary from the farms of Karbala. See Ràuf, tārīkh hawādith Baghdad wal-Basrah, p. 181. This affluence diminished by the end of Ahmed pāshā's rule in 1160/1747. However, ʿabd al-Rahman al-Suwaidi established some relationship with later Mamluk rulers, such as Omar pāshā and Sulayman al-Kabir. See Longrigg, Four centuries of modern Iraq, p. 257.
12 Al-Suwaidi's first long poem, composed at the age of twenty-two, was dedicated to Ahmad pāshā. Also the books ḥadīqat al-Zawrā' fī sīrat al-wuzarā' and tārīkh ḥawādith Baghdad wa al-Basra are examples of these writings. See Khulusi, tārīkh Baghdad. Also see Ràuf, tārīkh ḥawādith Baghdad wa al-Basra.
13 He also wrote about fiqh (jurisprudence), wisdom, Sufism, Arabic grammar and astronomy. For a full list of al-Suwaidi's writings, see Ràuf, tārīkh ḥawādith Baghdad wa al-Basra, pp. 32–36.
14 Al-Suwaidi wrote this book as a gift to the Mamluks' wālī, Hasan pāshā, who ruled Baghdad between 1778 and 1780. Al-Suwaidi, who was fifty-one years old at that time, considered it one of the hardest times in his life, as disease affected his friends, and the terrible situation forced him to leave.

15 He managed to send his family back to Baghdad, while he stayed in Basra for another two and a half years.

16 He was buried in the cemetery of Màruf al- Karkhi. See Ràuf, *tārīkh ḥawādith Baghdad wa al-Basra*, p. 31.

17 A city south of Baghdad, about 150 kilometres south-west of Baghdad.

18 Al-Amin, *'àyān al-shi'a.*

19 Al-Tamimi's poems were amazing to the extent that people started to call him Abu Tammam of the era. Abu Tammam al-Tài was a famous poet in the ninth century during the Abbasids' period. He was born in Egypt but lived in Baghdad for some time. He was also known for improvised yet eloquent poems that were full of enthusiasm and passion.

20 He was buried in al-Kazimiyya in the western side of Baghdad, 12 kilometres north of *al-Karkh.*

21 Cultural fora are special gatherings that are organised weekly. This phenomenon became more effective in Baghdad in the nineteenth century. These fora were held either at schools and mosques or at large houses that have a specific area for this purpose. People discuss different matters, including scientific, political and social matters. They also share poems and other writings.

22 Among the outstanding strategies in al-'Uzari's poetry is the use of symbolic meaning of scientific facts to describe the ethics of a person or to refer to some events. He praised community leaders, like Sulayman and 'abd-Allah al-Shawi. Those people were powerful, knowledgeable and respected leaders who had great relationships with the Arabic clans around Baghdad, yet they did not hold official positions in the government of Baghdad. With their bravery, nobility and wisdom, they acted as a means of communication in conflicts, and participated in solving problems in Baghdad. Historians note al-'Uzari's relationship with these leaders became stronger after his return from Hajj in 1161/1748. This explains his dedication to conciliation, at a time of increasing conflicts between the Mamluks over the governance of Baghdad. See Shukur, *diwān al-'Uzari al-Kabīr*, pp. 25–26. Also see Ràuf, *tārīkh ḥawādith Baghdad wa al-Basra*, p. 87.

23 Shukur, *diwān al-'Uzari al-Kabīr*, pp. 59–60. The Arabic script:

لاتنس ذكر أهلّة الزوراء	وأذا ذكرت حديث ريرب ضارج
فوران غيث من عيون سماء	بلد يفور الحسن من جنباته
شرقت بماء الدّمية الأدماء	هي بلدة أم جنّة أم وجنة
فيعود في الدّوحة الخضراء	ياأهل ودّي هل يفيء زماننا
مابين سألفتي سنى و سناء	حي اللّويلات التي سلفت لنا

24 Social beauty is the beauty of social gathering with family, friends and good people.

25 This leader is called 'As'ad al-Fakhri, who was a dignified scholar in Baghdad. See Shukur, *diwān al-'Uzari al-Kabīr*, p. 52.

26 Shukur, *diwān al-'Uzari al-Kabīr*, p. 355. The Arabic script:

ويشفى بريقه المعسول	قمر يقمر الفؤاد بمرآه
من عذاريه بالنّسيم البليل	نفحتنا منه الصبا فأتتنا

27 Baghdad used to have a wall on the river banks, but in the late seventeenth century, the governor of Baghdad ordered the demolition of that part and opened the city to the river.

28 Råuf, *tārīkh ḥawādith Baghdad wa al-Basra*, pp. 41–42. The Arabic script:

"ولمّا حلّ في هذه البقاع الطّاعون، وانقرض الرّجال الصّالحون، ووسّد الأمر الى غير أهله، ووضع كلّ
شيء في غير محلّه، زالت تلك المحاسن، وشربنا بعد الصّفاء من الأكدار الماء الآسن، فكأنّ تلك الأيّام
كانت سحابا ثم انقشع، وسرابا بلغ ثم انقطع، وكأنّ تلك الليالي كانت أحلاما، وتلك المحاسن كانت
مناما، أو كأنّها ظل امتدّ ثم ارتدّ، أو خيال طرق ثم انطلق، أو نبات نجم ثم انصرم، فتأمّلت هذه الدّنيا
في ائتلافها واختلافها، ومواتها وانحرافها، ووجدت وصالها فراقا، ونفاقها نفاقا، وماءها زعاقا،
وأملاكها طلاقا"

29 Råuf, *tārīkh ḥawādith Baghdad wa al-Basra*, p. 51. The Arabic script:

فقدّم لي أبا فرج النّياقا	الى بغداد أشتاق اشتياقا
ولاتنظر لمسراك الرّفاقا	وسر بي في ظلام الليل عسفا
اذا ما الأمر كان عليه ضاقا	فمثلي غير منتظر رفيقا
وقد بلغت من المقة الفواقا	ذكرت أحبّتي فازداد شوقي

30 This Arabic word indicates a metaphoric expression of suffering that is associated
with the loss of the soul during death and the impossibility of getting back to life.

31 Al-Qurʾan, Chapter 38, verse 15. The use of these meanings from the Qurʾan
indicates the great knowledge of and attachment to the Qurʾanic teachings at
that time.

32 Al-Amin, *ʿáyān al-shiʿa*. The Arabic poem:

وهام ما بين أغوار وأنجاد	صبّ تنقّل من واد إلى وادي
لا يملأ العين آلّا حسن بغداد	والحسن لا يتناهى في الورى وأرى

33 Al-Amin, *ʿáyān al-shiʿa*. The Arabic poem:

وعد من الله بل عهد وميثاق	في منكب الأرض للسّاعين أرزاق
انّ المقيم بها للخلد سبّاق	لا مهبط الوحي بغداد ولا ذكروا

34 As outlined previously, the round city was on the western side of Baghdad.

35 Råuf, *ʾakhbaar Baghdad*, p. 107.

36 Råuf, *tārīkh ḥawādith Baghdad wa al-Basra*, pp. 25–26. The Arabic script:

والشّمل مجتمع والسّعد تاويه	عهدي به وهو محفوف بكل هنا
والورد والآس تاها في نواحيه	والنّور والنّور في أرجائه سطعا
ممّا على الأرض عطر كامن فيه	وللصّبا أرج تحيا النّفوس به
والغصن بالخود يزري في تثنّيه	والطّير فوق أصول البان في طرب

37 Shukur, *diwān al-ʿUzari al-Kabīr*, p. 19. The Arabic script:

نعمنا وحيّاها من المزن صيّب	سلام على تلك المغاني التي بها
وقومي ترضى اذ رضيت وتغضب	اذا الكرخ داري والأحبّة جيرتي

38 Råuf, *tārīkh ḥawādith Baghdad wa al-Basra*, p. 25. The Arabic script:

"وقد انتبهت سحر بعض الليالي فاشتقت الى الكرخ وصلاة الفجر بين هاتيك الأطلال، فجرى دمعي توأما
وكاد أن يكون دما"

39 Råuf, *tārīkh ḥawādith Baghdad wa al-Basra*, pp. 25–26. The Arabic poem:

واسأله كيف خلت منه غوانيه	عرّج على الكرخ وانزل في مغانيه
وجملة الصّحب كانوا في نواديه	عهدي به وهو معمور بسادته
آثاره وخوت منه أعاليه	فماله ذهبت أصحابه وعفت
فجانب الشّرق طيبا لايدانيه	لهفي على الجانب الغربي أجمعه
ولم تزل من صدى التّفريق ترويه	بالله قف بدلي فيه كسارية
حيث العقيق على الخدّين أجريه	وقف وقوفي به يوم الرّحيل ضحى

40 Makkiyya, *Baghdad*, p. 283.

41 Ahmad Susa notes that in the eighteenth century, the lack of maintenance of the old dams caused recurrent overflows, which brought great damage to the urban landscape. See Susa, 'Ray Baghdad, qadiman wa hadithan', pp. 86–123.

42 Cooperson, 'Baghdad in rhetoric and narrative', pp. 99–113.

43 *'Eid* is a special happy event for Muslims. The two major annual *'Eid* are associated with fasting and Hajj.

44 Shukur, *diwan al-'Uzari al-Kabīr*, p. 501. The Arabic script:

والأرض راقصة بساكنها   فرحا بمالئها من النّعم
كلّ الجميل نتاج همّته   ان الرّياض ولائد الدّيم

45 Shukur, *diwān al-'Uzari al-Kabīr*, pp. 198–205. The Arabic script:

خلت الدّيار من الّذين عهدتهم   وتنافرت ظبيات ذاك الوادي
لله أندية النّسيم تعلّقت   أذياله بيشام ذاك النّادي
لولا العيون البابليّة وبحها   لم تعرف الأيّام كيف قيادي
سنحت لنا بين الفرات ودجلة   هيف المعاطف مشيهنّ تهادي

46 Rȧuf, *tārīkh ḥawādith Baghdad wa al-Basra*, p. 51. The Arabic poem:

ذكرت الخلد والأرواح تجري   به والماء يندفق اندفاقا
فهل من شربة أطفي غرامي   بها من ماء دجلة حيث راقا

47 Al-Amin, *'ȧyān al-shi'a*. The Arabic poem:

فلست أدري أهنّي ساكنيه به   بسائرات القوافي أم أهنّيه
فعاد يختال تيها في شبيبته   من بعد شيب علّى كبر يقاسيه
يصبو لدجلة مذ كانت مصافية   والمرء يصبو لمعشوق يصافيه

48 Al-Amin, *'ȧyān al-shi'a*. The Arabic poem:

يصبو إلى الدجلة العذراء عن شغب   يفري السباسب من ميل إلى ميل

49 Niebuhr, *Travels through Arabia and other countries in the East*.

50 Al-Suwaidi narrates an incident when the bridge was inoperative for about a month because of the damage of one of its thirty-four boats. See Rȧuf, *tārīkh ḥawādith Baghdad wa al-Basra*, p. 107.

51 *Tihāmah* refers to the Red Sea coastal plain of Arabia. It is also among the names of Makkah.

52 Shukur, *diwān al-'Uzari al-Kabīr*, p. 200. The Arabic script:

وبعثت من أقصى جبال تهامة   عرفا فضمّخ جانبي بغداد

53 Shukur, *diwān al-'Uzari al-Kabīr*, p. 179. The Arabic script:

ياصاحبي ان كنت تجهل ماالردى   فقف المطيّ بجانبي بغداد

54 Rȧuf, *tārīkh ḥawādith Baghdad wa al-Basra*, p. 105. The Arabic script:

"ومن جملة ماأرادوه من المكر بنا أن أرادوا احراق الجسر ليلا بأن يوجّهوا اليه قفافا خفية فيها رجال منهم ومعهم نار يلقونها في السفن. فيحترق الجسر وينقطع الطريق"

55 Rȧuf, *tārīkh ḥawādith Baghdad wa al-Basra*, p. 106. The Arabic script:

"فدبّت الحميّة فينا وعبرنا بالسّفن، وساعدنا قومنا الشرقيّين . . . ولم تمض ساعة من النّهار الا والجسر قد نصب، ووضعنا مكان سفنه الأربع أربع سفن من سفن أهل جانبنا"

56 Rȧuf, *'akhbaar Baghdad*, p. 140.

57 Rảuf, *al-ʿiqd al-lāmiʿ bi-ʾāthār Baghdad wal-masājid wal-jawāmiʿ*, p. 328.
   The Arabic script:

على ربعه كرها وسلّ حسامه   وجامع جسر جرّد الدّهر جيشه

الى شرف قدما أراش سهامه   الى ان تولّى الأمر داود زاده

58 Dawud *pāshā* was the last Mamluk ruler of Iraq, from 1816 to 1831.
59 Hamadeh, 'Public spaces and the garden culture of Istanbul in the eighteenth
   century', p. 281.
60 Rảuf, *al-ʿiqd al-lāmiʿ*, p. 140.
61 Al-Baheth al-Arabi, viewed 3 June 2013, term=روضة
62 Shukur, *diwān al-ʿUzari al-Kabīr*, pp. 153–154. The Arabic script:

ظفرت بأيّ وقاية بغداد   يامن وقى بغداد كلّ كريهة

فأصابه بعد الضّلال رشاد   كانت كركب تاه في سريانه

بها الأرواح والأجساد   بل روضة للخير لاهوتيّة تحيا

63 Shukur, *diwān al-ʿUzari al-Kabīr*, pp. 122–123. The Arabic script:

أين منّي نسيمه الفيّاح   ياشجا القلب أين روض المنى أم

غاب عن أفقنا به القّاح   زار أفق السماء ريحان فجر

64 Shukur, *diwān al-ʿUzari al-Kabīr*, pp. 203–205. The Arabic script:

والخصب في الأمطار شيء عادي   أمطرتم جفني فأخصب لي الضنى

كيف اختلاف الرّوض والرّوّاد   هذي المنازل فانزلاها تنظّرا

65 Al-ʾAlusi, *Baghdad fī al-shiʿr al-ʿarabī*, p. 157. The Arabic script:

ماأحرق القلب منّي شجو شجواك   لولاك يابلدة الزّوراء لولاك

سحب الكرائم في التّكريم محياك   سقى أديم الثّرى منك الحيا وحبت

زالت زهورك في صيف ومشتاك   واخضرّ ربعك من دون الرّبيع ولا

66 This is just a prediction by the author, as the poem draws a picture of stability
   in all scopes.
67 The Arabic word *sundus* refers to the fine delicate beautiful fabric mentioned in
   the Qurʾan, prepared especially for people in paradise.
68 The name of the angel Ridwan is associated with paradise, because Prophet
   Muhammad stated this angel guards the doors to paradise.
69 Al-Amin, *ʾáyān al-shiʿa*. The Arabic script:

فألبست نسج حمراء وصفراء   أروضة سقيت من صوب وطفاء

مسكا تضوّع من أردان عفراء   أبدت لنا كلّما مرّ النّسيم بها

من بعد ماصنعت فيها يد الماء   أظنّ سندس رضوان بجنّته

70 Mitchell, *Colonising Egypt*, p. 82.
71 Rảuf, *tārīkh ḥawādith Baghdad wa al-Basra*, p. 52.
72 Shukur, *diwān al-ʿUzari al-Kabīr*, p. 118. The Arabic script:

ظماً فبورك رأي كل ملجّج   والعلم لجّ لايصيب وفوده

مالجوهر النوري كالثّقل الدجي   كن كيف شئت مكوكبا أو مركزا

73 Shukur, *diwān al-ʿUzari al-Kabīr*, pp. 361–362. The Arabic script:

وعناصر الأشياء لم تتحوّل   لم تدر أنّك للمكارم عنصر

والرّوح موجبة قيام الهيكل   لك حكمة قام الوجود بلطفها

74 Al-Sàdi, *diwān shaykh Kazim al-ʾUzari al-Baghdadi*, p. 23. The Arabic script:

حدث عن السعد لانكر ولاعجب · فالسعد بحر من الاقدار منسكب
لولا ملاحظة الأفلاك من صعد · ماكان قلب الحديد الصّلّب ينجذب

75 Shukur, *diwān al-ʾUzari al-Kabīr*, p. 90. The Arabic script:

وأرى الحياة لذيذة لكنها · ربما تملّ لفرقة الأحباب
قم ننهب السّاعات في طلب العلى · وتناس ذكر سوالف الأحقاب

76 Ràuf, *tārīkh ḥawādith Baghdad wa al-Basra*, p. 83. The Arabic script:

''العالم العلّامة والحبر الفهّامة'' صاحب التّحقيقات العديدة والتّصنيفات المفيدة''

77 Ràuf, *tārīkh ḥawādith Baghdad wa al-Basra*, p. 44. The Arabic script:

''فأعجبني اشتغالهم وتأنّست بهم وتأنّسوا بي''

78 Ràuf, *tārīkh ḥawādith Baghdad wa al-Basra*, p. 46.

79 For more details about the trip of al-Suwaidi, see Ràuf, *tārīkh ḥawādith Baghdad wa al-Basra*.

80 Ràuf, *tārīkh ḥawādith Baghdad wa al-Basra*, p. 51. The Arabic script:

''وبعد أيّام قليلة انفتح طريق بغداد . . . فأرسلت الجميع في سفينة, وبقيت وحدي. وليس في البصرة
من طلبة العلم باقيا من حرب الطاعون سوى السّيد ياسين . . . فلذلك كنت أشتاق الى بغداد''

81 Ràuf, *tārīkh ḥawādith Baghdad wa al-Basra*, p. 41. The Arabic script:

''أعلم اي أخي . . . فبغداد والبصرة وما والاهما كان أهلها بالنسبة الى غيرهما قبل حلول الطاعون
فيهما في أرغد عيش وأهناه, وأعدل وقت وأعلاه''

82 Ghaidan, 'Damage to Iraqi's wider heritage', p. 85.

83 According to Ràuf, this building survived until 1961 when it was demolished and replaced with another mosque, which still exists. See Ràuf, *al-ʾiqd al-lāmiʾ*, p. 116.

84 This is a metaphoric example where the poet compares the new mosque to the Kaʾba. He refers to some places near Makkah that should be visited during Hajj, like Mina and Muzdalifah (Muhassab).

85 Ràuf, *al-ʾiqd al-lāmiʾ*, p. 115. The Arabic script:

هو البيت لو أن المحصّب أو منى · بجنبيه لم تقطع الى البيت شاسعا
اذا حلّ جبّار قرارة صحنه · غدا قلبه من خشية الله طائعا
اذا جئت للزّوراء قف عند بابها · ترى جامعا من غفلة الجهل مانعا

86 Ràuf, *al-ʾiqd al-lāmiʾ*, p. 517. The Arabic script:

فعج الى الكرخ ترى مسجدا · قد أورفت بالعفو أفنانه
وأرّخن أكرم به مسجدا · على تقى أسّس بنيانه

87 Ràuf, *al-ʾiqd al-lāmiʾ*, p. 387. The Arabic script:

ذي بركة يرتوي منها بضحضاح · كادت تؤلّف ابدانا بأرواح
فصبغة الله اجرى ماءها غدقا · للواردين بتدبير وأصلاح
ان جئت ظمأن قلب يامؤرّخها · اشرب هنيئا مرينا بارد الرّاح

88 Waqf is a non-transferable endowment in Islamic law, typically denoting a building or plot of land for religious or charitable purposes. The donated assets are held by a charitable trust.

89 For more information about cultural fora, see Al-Durubi, *al-baghdādiyyūn, ʾakhbāruhum wa majālisuhum.*

90 Al-Durubi, *al-baghdādiyyūn, ʾakhbāruhum wa majālisuhum,* p. 354.

91 Râuf, *al-ʿiqd al-lāmiʿ,* p. 86. The Arabic script:

حيّ هذي القبور ان كنت حيّا   عاملا بالفضيلة الغرّاء

انما الميت كلّ من لا يحيي   باحترام مقابر الشّهداء

واحترام الأموات حتم وان كا   نوا بعادا فكيف بالقرباء

انّما هذه القبور ترينا   كيف حبّ الأوطان في الأحياء

92 Râuf, *al-ʿiqd al-lāmiʿ,* p. 20. The Arabic script:

"كان في موضع بغداد قرية تسمى باسمها، وكانت تقام فيها سوق عظيمة في كلّ شهر فيأتيها التّجار من فارس والأهواز وسائر البلاد . . . ففي سنة 13 من الهجرة . . . المثنى الشّيباني . . . قال له: أريد أن أغير على سوق بغداد"

93 Inalcik & Quataert, *An economic and social history of the Ottoman Empire,* p. 696.

94 Râuf, *al-ʿiqd al-lāmiʿ,* p. 490. The Arabic script:

زاوية واقعة في محلة سوق الجديد، ويسمى سوق اللبن، وسمّي سوق الجديد لأنشائه حديثا، وسوق اللبن "لكون اللبن يباع فيه"

95 For example, Abadah identifies the shoe market that lies next to Jamiʿ al-Wazir: "The *yamanchiyya* are the people who make the Yamani [a red shoe الخف الأحمر that was used since early Islamic days], and they have a special market in Baghdad". See Râuf, *al-ʿiqd al-lāmiʿ,* p. 251. The Arabic script:

"واليمنجيّة هم عاملوا الأحذية، اليمني، لهم سوق مخصوص في بغداد"

96 These decorations usually take place on the happy occasions. For example, the birth of a new baby for the *pāshā,* or when they gain a victory in a battle. Khulusi, *tārīkh Baghdad,* p. 37.

97 An example of these *khans* that have retail shops is *khan* Jighal, which was originally built in 999/1590, and was reported among the properties of Sulayman *pāshā* in 1206/1792, as having many shops that were occupied by jewellers. See Râuf, *tārīkh ḥawādith Baghdad wa al-Basra,* p. 120.

98 Shukur, *diwān al-ʿUzari al-Kabīr,* p. 434. The Arabic script:

يهنيك ياكربلا وشي ظفرت به   من صنعة اليُمن لا من صنعة اليَمن

من مبلغ سوق ذاك اليوم انّ به   جواهر القدس قد بيعت بلا ثمن

99 This tragedy took place in 61/680 when Imam Hussein, the grandson of Prophet Muhammad, was killed along with his family and companions.

100 This poem is dedicated to praise ʾAsʿad Fakhri Zadah (d. 1203/1788).

101 Shukur, *diwān al-ʿUzari al-Kabīr,* p. 323. The Arabic script:

معاهد حلّتهن مصر بوشيها   وأهدت اليهنّ التصاوير فارس

شروني على علم بأبخس قيمة   وللحبّ نقد للمحبّين باخس

102 Râuf, *tārīkh ḥawādith Baghdad wa al-Basra,* pp. 134–135. The Arabic script:

"ففي بعض الليالي رأى حارس من حرّاس الأسواق بعض السوقة جاؤوا ليلا، وأخرجوا مالهم من دكاكينهم . . . فلما أصبح الصّباح صار الميدان كالعادة، كل ذي حرفة مشغول بحرفته، وكأنهم لم يشعروا بما وقع ليلا"

103 ʿUmar *pāshā* was the *wālī* of Baghdad at that time.

104 Råuf, *tārīkh ḥawādith Baghdad wa al-Basra*, p. 66. The Arabic script:

"فاتصل بعمر باشا ودله على مظالم . . . وجرأه على أخذ أموال الناس حتى هربت من جوره أكثر التجار
في الأمصار الشاسعة والأقطار الواسعة . . . ولما اتصل بعبد الله باشا وصار عنده خزندارا هرب جميع
تجار بغداد بعيالهم وأموالهم، وامتنعت تجار الأطراف من الدخول الى بغداد"

105 Råuf, *al-ʿiqd al-lāmiʿ*, p. 518. The Arabic script:

سماؤه بالخنّس الكنّس   أقسم بالله الذي زيّنت

ذو همّة بالفلك الأطلس   انّ الذي شيّد هذا البنا

من ناطق فيه ومن أخرس   فقل لمن يجهد في مكسب

أرّخ وبالميزان لاتبخسِ   أوف أذا كلت ومن بعد ذا

106 Hamadeh, 'Public spaces and the garden culture of Istanbul in the eighteenth century', p. 299.

107 See Al-Rumaythi, 'maqāhi Baghdad', viewed 3 June 2013, <https://sites. google.com/site/elkarbalaee/baghdadcoffieshops>. Also, Råuf suggested the first coffee shop was built in Baghdad in *khan* Jighal but the date was 899/1590 instead.

108 Al-Janabi, 'tārīkh Baghdad yastarkhī fī ḍilāl maqhā al-Khaffāfīn', viewed 3 June 2013, <www.aljanabi.com>.

109 Al-Rumaythi, 'maqāhi Baghdad'.

110 Al-Durubi, *al-baghdādiyyūn, ʾakhbāruhum wa majālisuhum*, p. 346.

111 By mid-twentieth century, the educational role of coffee shops weakened, but they maintained their entertainment function. At present, they are diminishing in Baghdad as they have been gradually replaced with other shops and clubs. However, a number of historical *maqhās* still exist actively.

112 The poet only mentioned wine symbolically, though drinking alcohol is forbidden in Islam and no religious scholar would take it.

113 Shukur, *diwān al-ʿUzari al-Kabīr*, p. 470. The Arabic script:

هي القهوة السّوداء فا نعم بشرخها   ودع عنك شمطاء طوتها دهورها

فأنّ بياض العين للعين ظلمة   وأنّ سواد العين للعين نورها

114 Al-Baheth al-Arabi, viewed 3 June 2013, <http://www.baheth.info/all.jsp?term=قهوة>

115 Another example of the interpretation of colours was explained in Chapter 3, in the poetry of al-Hilli.

116 Råuf, *tārīkh ḥawādith Baghdad wa al-Basra*, p. 116. The Arabic script:

"ونهبوا خانات البقاقيل التي في دقاقين القهوة. وأخذوا جميع مافيها من توتون وعفص وصابون"

117 Råuf, *tārīkh ḥawādith Baghdad wa al-Basra*, p. 118. The Arabic script:

"فرتّبنا لهم المشاعل والقهوة والتوتون كل ليلة، وجعلنا طعامهم صباحا ومساء على جانبنا أربعة أيام"

118 ʿRåuf, *tārīkh ḥawādith Baghdad wa al-Basra*, p. 135. The Arabic script:

"
فجاءا الى الميدان فأبصرا القهوة خانة التي عند باب القلعة غاصة بالرجال والسلاح، ثم أبصرا عند باب
الأمام الأعظم مثل ذلك، وذهبا الى ناحية محمّد الفضل فوجدا ثمّة مثل ذلك"

119 The word *qahwa* is a substitute to the word *maqhā* in Iraqi terms.

120 For more examples, see Ra'of, *al-ʿiqd al-lāmiʿ*.

121   Rảuf (ed.), *al-ʿiqd al-lāmiʿ*, p. 329. The Arabic script:

بغداد حسنا يروق العين واضحه   آثار داود آثار بها لبست
ويكره الضّيق غاديه ورائحه   تشكو الرصافة قدما ضيق مسلكها
وباب جسر حبي بالنّصر مانحه   فأمنحت بطريق لا زحام له

122   Shukur, *diwān al-ʿUzari al-Kabīr*, p. 249. The Arabic script:

يادار لابعدت قبابك عن فتى   سدّ البعاد عليه كل سداد

123   Shukur, *diwān al-ʿUzari al-Kabīr*, pp. 198–205. The Arabic script:

يحمى النّزيل بها ويروى الصّادي   هل بعد أندية الحمى من ناد
بئس الوفاء لذلك الميعاد   وعدوا الرّحيل عشيّة ووفوا به
تلك القباب عريب ذاك الوادي   وخلا العذيب فما خلا مذ قوّضت

124   The poet does not mean sacrificing his father literally, but symbolically. He points out the dignity and high ethics of those people, to a degree that one would sacrifice his most precious people for their sake.

125   Shukur, *diwān al-ʿUzari al-Kabīr*, pp. 111–112. The Arabic script:

سمكوا لها فلكا من الفيروزج   بأبي الأهلّة في القباب كأنّما
هذا النّسيم نسيمهم فتأرّجي   وأقول للأرض التي ذكروا بها

126   Rảuf, *tārīkh ḥawādith Baghdad wa al-Basra*, pp. 41–42. The original Arabic poem:

"ورأيت المغترّ بها على شرف غرر، والعجب بنعيمها على شفا خطر، والمتعلّق بحبالها كالمتعلّق بنسيج العناكب بل بأوهن منه وأوهى، والسّاكن الى قبابها كمعانق الأسد بل أجنّ وأجنى"

127   Rảuf, *al-ʿiqd al-lāmiʿ*, p. 243. The Arabic script:

للذّاكرين بتسبيح وتحميد   ذا من بيوت بأذن الله قد رفعت
ذو العلم والحلم والأنصاف والجود   على تقى الله بالأخلاص أسّسه

128   Shukur, *diwān al-ʿUzari al-Kabīr*, pp. 53–56. The Arabic script:

نشرت جناحيها به السّرّاء   ولقد ذكرت بذي الأراكة منزلا
والدّوح ترقص تحته الأفياء   ومذانب الغدران يطفح ماؤها
ولو استجارت فيهم الأعداء   يحمى نزيلهم ويأمن جارهم

129   This is one of the verses in the Qurʾan: "and We started every living creature from water" Chapter 21, verse 30.

130   Shukur, *diwān al-ʿUzari al-Kabīr*, p. 191. The Arabic script:

مطالع سعد أو مطارح جود   لعمري خلت تلك الديار ولم تزل
سوى أنّها ليست بدار خلود   كأنّ من الفردوس روضة ظلّها

131   Shukur, *diwān al-ʿUzari al-Kabīr*, p. 238. The Arabic script:

عقرت بعهدك كوم كل عهاد   يادار من عقرت عليه مودّتي
مشي الأسير بأثقل الأصفاد   وتمشّت النّسمات فيك عليلة

132   Shukur, *diwān al-ʿUzari al-Kabīr*, pp. 172–173. The Arabic script:

حتى استحال بها كلانا أرمدا   في ليلة ساهرت كوكب أفقها
بحياتهم هات الحديث المسندا   يانسمة الوادي الذي نزلوا بهم

133 Shukur, *diwān al-ʿUzari al-Kabīr*, pp. 203–206. The Arabic script:

من لي بعود كواكب سيّارة   محمودة في مبدأ ومعاد
قمر يذكّرني به قمر الدّجى   قد تذكر الأشياء بالأنداد

134 Makkiyya, *Baghdad*, p. 286.

135 Rảuf, *tārīkh ḥawādith Baghdad wa al-Basra*, p. 75. The Arabic script:

لما جئت من البصرة الى بغداد من العجم هاربا، والى رؤية أصحابي وأحبابي راغبا، رأيت أحبابي قد
أبادهم الطاعون، اباد معهم سائر أهل الفضل . . فأثرت مذهب العزلة والأنفراد، واخترت طريقة النأي
والبعاد، وقعدت في البيت وحدي، واشتغلت بالكتب التي عندي"

136 Rảuf, *tārīkh ḥawādith Baghdad wa al-Basra*, p. 79. The Arabic script:

"فالشّرع والرأي انا لانكون مع أحد, وبغداد لاتأتي الا لوزير عظيم"

137 Rảuf, *tārīkh ḥawādith Baghdad wa al-Basra*, p. 76. The Arabic script:

لم أجد لذّة في السلامة إلا   صرت للبيت والكتاب جليسا

138 These houses contained typical domestic facilities, in addition to particular places to cool water for drinking. Underground rooms were mainly used in summer.

139 Rảuf, *ʾakhbaar Baghdad*, p. 122.

140 Rảuf, *ʾakhbaar Baghdad*, p. 115.

141 ʿAbd al-Baqi al-ʿUmari is a prominent Iraqi poet. He was born in Mosul north Baghdad in 1204/1789, and he lived in Baghdad for a while. He died in Baghdad in 1278/1870, and he left behind a great poetry collection. See Rảuf, *ʾakhbaar Baghdad*, p. 114.

142 Rảuf, *ʾakhbaar Baghdad*, p. 116. The Arabic script:

رواق شهاب الدين في العزّ معقود   به العلم مشهور به الفضل مشهود
بغرفته كم غرفة لمؤمّل   كأنّ نهر طالوت بهاتيك معهود
لقد حسدت زهر النجوم تخومه   وكل رفيع القدر في الكون محسود

143 Rảuf, *ʾakhbaar Baghdad*, p. 117. The Arabic script:

"هي دار لطيفة الوضع, بديعة السّمت، محكمة البناء، واسعة الفناء، وقد أنشأ فيها غرفة تحاكي غرف
الجنان، مزخرفة السّقف والجدران"

144 The Arabic word Saʿid means 'happy', that's why the poet described Saʿid al-Mufti a happy man in this life and the hereafter.

145 Rảuf, *ʾakhbaar Baghdad*, p. 118. The Arabic script:

بسعيد الدّارين بنيت دارا   ميّزتها أنظاره بمزايا
أسعد النّاس حلّها وسعيد   فأمنّا بها حلول الرّزايا
هي والله للفضائل مأوى   كم خبايا منها تقلّ الزوايا

146 Rảuf, *ʾakhbaar Baghdad*, p. 113. The Arabic script:

دمية القصر هذه أم عروس   قلّدتها نجومها الجوزاء
وتجلّت حين انجلت فتجلّت   بحلاها وحلّيها الزّوراء

Summary

This book endeavoured to promote the understanding of Baghdad's urban history through reading and interpreting texts. It investigated poetry and narratives composed in different periods starting from the founding of the round city of Baghdad and ending with the nineteenth century. The examination of the history of literature and poetry in Baghdad indicates fluctuating conditions, contingent upon variable circumstances. These conditions are reflected greatly in the intellectual products. The use of textual representation proved the validity of this technique in understanding the complex history of Baghdad, due to the great capacity of texts to reveal the hidden ideas of the past. The demonstration of the literary activity in Baghdad proved the intensity of writings despite recurrent political problems. Although the material structure of Baghdad has been sketched out through conventional resources, the analysis of literature and poetry in this book highlighted other ways to understand architectural and urban components of the city. These methods enabled us to view conventional forms differently and to recognise meanings related to other forms of knowledge.

The analysis of urban literature entails an understanding of the ideas embedded in texts, and involves examining knowledge of the language used in them. Although these ideas usually exist throughout the whole text, they are, at the same time, concealed in the body of the text and cannot be accessed with ease. The method of reading texts – integrated interpretation – assisted in accessing these ideas and proved valid in searching for a more comprehensive meaning of place. This method utilised diverse interpretations of historical texts, as well as interconnection and comparison of different periods in history. Interconnection is the most effective key objective, which intermingles ideas and spaces, of internal and external meanings, as a factual quality of life that should be emphasised in historical studies to advance the understanding of the past. The rich outcomes of this textual representation confirms the unique role of the interpretation of urban literature in providing fruitful ideas that may change our perspective on history and help to expand our methods of historical writing.

Integrated interpretation focused on the thematic approach as an initial tool for examination that underlines particular qualities of the city and reveals the implications of texts towards the evaluation of architectural meaning, in addition to the investigation of distinctive notions of the urban history of Baghdad. This approach involved horizontal interpretation that employs interconnection and comparison, in addition to vertical interpretation that utilises double interpretation of texts to obtain the general meaning across multiple texts first and then interpret single texts to elaborate that meaning. In this way, vertical interpretation established continuity in historical connotations. However, the cumulative approach is also utilised to enrich the meaning, by interpreting single words first and moving to the whole text.

Love and affection towards Baghdad was presented in literature written by both residents and visitors. Given that nostalgia fashioned writing modes in the literature of Baghdadis, nostalgic themes of love, affection and attachment generated composite concepts related to the philosophical connections between people and place in history, which helped to identify meanings of the past. In addition to nostalgic themes, literary analyses noted a celebration of the spatial themes of the city. By engaging language, including rhetoric and metaphors to highlight spatial themes, these texts assisted in interpreting architectural meaning and re-evaluating historical forms in relation to their common understanding in history. Besides, the examination of reflective themes in texts highlighted important social aspects of Baghdad that are either not emphasised or misinterpreted in the available historical sources. For example, reflective expressions about the round city of Baghdad indicated unjust distribution of wealth and inequality. They also showed interesting human interrelationships in the eighteenth century and fascinating architecture combined with social connections in the nineteenth century.

The analysis of poetry revealed social consciousness and religious awareness, as well as architectural and urban perceptions. The adherence to the Islamic rules and the intense use of metaphorical meanings from the Qur'an shaped these texts. The expansive meanings of Arabic words enabled the writers to produce complicated texts that reflected a skilful use of the language. In its complexity, beauty in the literature of Baghdadi scholars correlates with Qur'anic perspectives and images. Expressions of beauty in these texts encased a profound spiritual beauty and were concerned with oneness, justice, guidance and wisdom, which are the core themes in the Qur'an. The writers reflected heavily on the attributes of God to gain meanings for their experiences. The implementation of new methods in writing and the plentiful amount of literature throughout the history of Baghdad indicate a continuous advancement of literature in general.

Among the unique dimensions of beauty that emerged from these interpretations were the meanings of social connection. It appears that the historical clash between constant beauty and transitory beauty mainly relates to physical features, which influence the understanding of urban history to a great extent. The interpretation of poetry showed the strong association of the phenomenon of beauty in Baghdad with social beauty. The poets described an extremely favourable atmosphere that referred to intellect, imagination and humour as major traits of beauty. While perfect social happiness was indicated in the first century of the establishment of the second settlement, undesirable social issues were outlined in the literature after two centuries of development. These notions and interrelationships remained the focus of the literature throughout the history of the city.

Since scholars and poets of Baghdad were the intermediary group (*ḥalaqa wasaṭiyya*) between public and political leaders, their writings expressed a great deal of their social context and approached architecture and everyday life within this context. Attachment to the city is indicated differently in texts depending on the circumstances of the writer and the aim of the piece of writing. On first examination, the poems seem to refer to matters that do not relate to architecture and urban research. The apparent purpose of writing seems to outline specific dialogue related to leadership, power and other aspects. Yet, upon closer inspection, these texts unveiled distinct thematic approaches to every aspect of history, including architecture. This suggests these texts to be historically momentous pieces for mapping out overlooked issues in the history of Baghdad, since understanding the experience of individuals and single groups can lead to the understanding of the history of other groups in society.

The examination of poetry and narratives affirmed the disparity between political and intellectual movements in history. Interpretation of urban literature disclosed more functions of historical recording other than legitimising authority, or predicting and controlling the future. This case proved that the understanding of cities is not limited to official or political documents. It verified that Baghdad effectively existed before the actual construction of the round city, since social relationships and market activity were the permanent identifiers of place. The interpretation of the city used a number of interconnected elements that contradicted gloomy images portrayed in conventional historical resources. These images employ physical structures as the only measure of beauty and refer to political complexities rather than social aspects of place. Therefore, we can conclude that the continuity of cities is related to social activity to a much greater extent than other meanings. Also, it is important to view literary development as a continuous action in history to prevent episodic or fragmentary perspectives that hinder the understanding of history.

The textual representation illustrated a mixture of positive and negative aspects in all periods. The reading of texts showed a remarkable situation of continuously changing character, with a frequent rise and decline of the city, highlighting deeper meanings of the city's history. The urban literature of the Abbasid era – which lasted for four and half centuries – fluctuated between expressing admiration for the city and complaining about social and economic problems, depending on the circumstances of the scholar, his individual experience and the conditions of the city in general. The few poems that mentioned the round city outlined negative features more than the positive. Conversely, the second settlement of Baghdad that emerged naturally and gradually has held a greater space in literature, with different perceptions. While some texts expressed great appreciation of this settlement, others viewed it as a place of injustice and misery. However, appreciation of the second settlement was expressed more than discontent. This range of expressions indicates realistic impressions of the city, since it is impossible to have fixed conditions of cities throughout history.

Among the unique characteristics of Baghdad that have been outlined in literature is the effective role of learning activity, which is articulated as a fixed historical feature of Baghdad. The widespread dissemination of knowledge in Baghdad emphasised strong human relations, which suggests a remarkable increase of learning activities, starting from the eleventh and twelfth centuries onward. These learning centres and intellectual activities made many scholars eager to reside there. The multiple functions of mosques and schools, their specific locations, and also their design standards presented their sociability within the larger public space. Apart from an extensive documentation of the structures of schools and mosques that represent learning centres in Baghdad, available historical sources do not highlight learning centres as a powerful component of place; rather they present them as a remnant of Baghdad's past.

The outcome of the texts' interrogation in this book uncovered a new perspective of Baghdad and of urban history studies in general. The Tigris River has been a major and eternal element of Baghdad's urban continuity throughout history. The interrelationship of this river with other urban components of Baghdad, such as mosques, in addition to parks, is among its distinctive qualities. The broad idea of public gardens that are interconnected with the river, and encompass other urban forms shows the crucial role of the river in urban life. These texts did not limit gardens to a specific locale, as they expressed multiple meanings of gardens that go beyond physical limits. Collective consciousness of multiple meaning of gardens that include aesthetic, psychological, social and spiritual qualities is among the remarkable aspect of urban literature interrogated in this book. Another urban feature of Baghdad that is interconnected with the river is Baghdad's markets that existed before the foundation of the round city and continued to exist until today. These markets survived through the profits of the river, and they continued to survive in Baghdad regardless of intermittent tragedies.

Although historical sources signify the period after the fall of Abbasids in the thirteenth century until the nineteenth century as a period of conflicts and recurrent disasters, this book proved otherwise. The plentiful writings and varying objectives demonstrate the continuous development of different aspects of society, including literature. Although urban development always runs parallel to the political line, it cannot be fully influenced by political issues. For example, the sixteenth century is considered as a century of extensive fights between the Ottomans and the Safavids over the control of Baghdad, though this century witnessed a great educational movement. Thus, it becomes clear that there is a neglected thread in conventional historiography. This thread represents social and cultural development of the city. The reading of the poetry and historical narratives of the eighteenth century constitutes exclusive spatial and nostalgic themes. These texts emphasise social beauty over other aspects and demonstrate the tragic consequences of epidemics, which diminished it. The image of the early nineteenth century is more contented, which suggests an equal increase in all measures of beauty. This reveals the solid links between all aspects of beauty, along with the great influence they have on each other.

The textual representation in the eighteenth and nineteenth centuries endeavoured to signify nostalgic and spatial themes that are unobserved in the historiography of Baghdad. The interpretation of the writings of Baghdadis in this period provided insight into the particular concerns of the society at that time, making them a valid historiographical source. They also contained depictions of the urban landscape of Baghdad and the particular qualities that contributed to its beauty. The poetry and narratives of al-ʾUzari, al-Suwaidi, al-Tamimi and others have guided the search to uncover these urban themes and spaces. These texts depicted architecture through similar metaphorical expressions and showed a parallel awareness and familiarity towards outlining their contexts. They also revealed previously unexamined assumptions about historical writing of this period. Each text highlighted unique conceptual details, which challenge conventional statements about the urban history of Baghdad.

Interpreting texts in this book enabled the relocation of architecture into a context where form was not determined by a single cause, and where human intelligence, in collaboration with environmental resources, was backed up by divine laws to produce these forms. This representation transformed architectural elements into the qualitative realm, interacting with other values to reveal love and affection for the city. The interlocking aspects of all elements of interpretation – including scientific and social criteria – presented a dynamic method which promoted a continuous interconnection between components of the past, and between the past and present.

Finally, this study provided evidence that successful historical analysis should always open up to other disciplines to gain greater meanings of the past. The collective representation of poetry, narratives and architectural documents attempted to discover the broader historical context, which does not rely on individuals or on particular incidents. Since all historical writings, in general, contain a mix of ideas, the use of the 'integrated interpretation' scheme along with scholarly judgement identified various ideas. Through recognising multiple literary sources of architectural and urban analysis, this book initiated another approach to historical writing. This was achieved by establishing effective means of integration that enhance particular qualities and assist in differentiating truthful and fictional concepts, while maintaining strong associations between different interpretations of the past.

Among the important outcomes of this study is the acknowledgement of the vital influence of attitudes on the writing of history. Perhaps the key aim of re-writing history should be to institute the elevation of knowledge as the ultimate goal of writing, instead of temporary, personal or political benefits. The interrelationship between architecture and different events reveals additional identifiers of place such as social connections, environmental awareness and learning perception. Moreover, it affirms the disparity between political and intellectual movements in history and provides evidence that successful historical analysis should always open up to other disciplines to gain greater meanings of the past.

Bibliography

English references

ʿAbdullah, T. 2001, *Merchants, Mamluks, and murder: The political economy of trade in eighteenth-century Basra*, SUNY series in the social and economic history of the Middle East, State University of New York Press, Albany, Britain.

Aga Khan Award for Architecture 1986, *Architectural education in the Islamic world: proceedings of seminar ten in the series: Architectural transformations in the Islamic world*, April 21–25, 1986, Granada, Spain, Concept Media Pte Ltd, Singapore.

Akkach, S. 2005, *Cosmology and architecture in pre-modern Islam: An architectural reading of mystical ideas*, SUNY series in Islam, State University of New York Press, Albany.

Al-Baghdadi, N. 2005 April, 'From heaven to dust: Metamorphosis of the book in pre-modern Arab culture', *The Medieval History Journal*, vol. 8, pp. 83–107.

Al-Duri, A. 1987, *The historical formation of the Arab nation: A study in identity and consciousness*, Croom Helm, London.

Atasoy, N. 2004, 'Ottoman garden pavilions and tents', in *Muqarnas*, vol. 21, Essays in Honor of J.M. Rogers, sponsored by The Aga Khan Program for Islamic Architecture at Harvard University and the Massachusetts Institute of Technology, Cambridge, Massachusetts, pp. 15–19.

Bianca, S. & Eidgenossische Technische Hochschule Zurich, Institut fur Orts-Regional- und Landesplanung 2000, *Urban form in the Arab world: Past and present*, VDF, Zurich.

Bonine, M.E. 2005, 'Islamic urbanism, urbanites, and the Middle Eastern city', in Choueiri, Y.M. (ed.), *A companion to the history of the Middle East, Blackwell companions to world history*, Blackwell Pub. Ltd, Malden, MA.

British Library, <www.bl.uk, Mss>. Add. 16561, folio 60, recto, dated 1468.

Cerasi, M. 2005, 'The urban and architectural evolution of the Istanbul divanyolu: Urban aesthetics and ideology in Ottoman town building', Muqarnas, vol. 22, pp. 189–232.

Cooperson, M. 1996, 'Baghdad in rhetoric and narrative', *Muqarnas: An Annual on the Visual Culture of the Islamic World, Volume 13: Aga Khan Program for Islamic Architecture*, pp. 99–113.

Crinson, M. 2003, *Modern architecture and the end of Empire*, Ashgate, Burlington, VT.

Fletcher, B. & Musgrove, J. 1987, *Sir Banister Fletcher's a history of architecture*, 19th edn, Butterworths, London, Boston, p. 532.

Gadamer, H.G. 1994, *Literature and philosophy in dialogue: Essays in German literary theory*, State University of New York Press, Albany.

——— 1997, *Truth and method*, 2nd rev. edn, Continuum, New York.

——— 2006, 'Language and understanding (1970)', *Theory, Culture, and Society*, vol. 23, pp. 13–27.

Ghaidan, U. 2008, 'Damage to Iraqi's wider heritage', in Stone, P.G., Farchakh, J. & Fisk, R. (eds.), *The destruction of cultural heritage in Iraq*, The heritage matters series, vol. 1, Boydell Press, Woodbridge, Suffolk.

Grabar, O. 1987, *The formation of Islamic art*, Rev. and enl. edn, Yale University Press, New Haven.

Hamadeh, Sh. 2007, 'Public spaces and the garden culture of Istanbul in the eighteenth century', in Aksan, V.H. & Goffman, D. (eds.), *The early modern Ottomans: Remapping the empire*, Cambridge University Press, Cambridge, NY.

Inalcik, H. & Quataert, D. 1997, *An economic and social history of the Ottoman Empire, Volume 2: 1600–1914*, 2 vols, Cambridge University Press, Cambridge, NY.

Kellner, H. 1985, 'Time and narrative by Paul Ricoeur; history and criticism by Dominick LaCapra', *MLN*, vol. 100, no. 5.

Kritzeck, J. 1964, *Anthology of Islamic literature, from the rise of Islam to modern times*, 1st edn, Holt, Rinehart, New York.

Lafi, N. 2007, 'The Ottoman municipal reforms between old regime and modernity: Towards a new interpretive paradigm', in Cihangir, E. (ed.), *Uluslararas Eminonu Sempozyumu: Tebligler kitab international symposium on eminonu: The book of notifications*, Eminonu Belediyesi Baskanlg, Istanbul.

Lassner, J. 1970, *The topography of Baghdad in the early middle ages: Text and studies*, Wayne State University Press, Detroit.

Lewis, B. & Thomas Leiper Kane Collection 1975, *History: Remembered, recovered, invented*, Princeton University Press, Princeton, NJ.

Longrigg, S.H. 1968, *Four centuries of modern Iraq*, Librairie du Liban, Beirut.

Mills, C.W. 1959, *The social imagination*, Oxford University Press, New York.

Mitchell, T. 1988, *Colonising Egypt*, Cambridge University Press, Cambridge, NY.

Moholy-Nagy, S. 1968, *Matrix of man: An illustrated history of urban environment*, Pall Mall Press, London.

Morkoc, S.B. 2008, 'Reading architecture from the text: The Ottoman story of the four marble columns', *Journal of Near Eastern Studies*, vol. 1, no. 67.

——— 2010, *A study of Ottoman narratives on architecture: Text, context and hermeneutics*, Academia Press, Bethesda.

Niebuhr, C. & Heron, R. 1792, *Travels through Arabia and other countries in the East*, R. Morison and Son, Edinburgh.

Raymond, R. 2005, 'Urban life and Middle Eastern cities: The traditional Arab city', in Choueiri, Y.M. (ed.), *A companion to the history of the Middle East*, Blackwell companions to world history, Blackwell Pub. Ltd, Malden, MA.

Said, E.W., Suleiman, F. & Association of Arab-American University Graduates 1973, *The Arabs today: Alternatives for tomorrow*, Forum Associates, Columbus, Ohio.

Smith, M. 1977, *An early mystic of Baghdad: A study of the life and teaching of Harith b. Asad Al-Muhasibi, A.D. 781-A.D. 857*, AMS Press, New York.

Tripp, C. 2007, *A history of Iraq*, 3rd edn, Cambridge University Press, Cambridge, NY.

Veinstein, G. 2008, 'The Ottoman town: Fifteenth-eighteenth centuries', in Jayyusi, S.K., Holod, R., Petruccioli, A. & Raymond, A. (eds.), *The city in the Islamic world*, Brill, Leiden, Boston, pp. 207–212.

Warren, J. & Fethi, I. 1982, *Traditional houses in Baghdad*, Coach Publishing House, Horsham, England.

Arabic references

Al-ʾAlusi, J.A. 1987, *Baghdad fī al-shiʾr al-ʿarabī: min tārīkhihā wa ʾakhbārihā al-ḥaḍāriyya* (Baghdad in the Arabic poetry), al-majmaʾ al-ʾilmi al-Iraqi, Baghdad.

Al-Amin, M. 1951, *ʾaʿyān al-shiʾa* (Notable shiʾa scholars), viewed 2 June 2013, <www.alseraj.net/a-k/rejal/ayan/1.pdf>.

Al-Baheth al-Arabi, <www.baheth.info>.

Al-Bustani, K. (ed.) 2009, *dīwān safiy al-dīn al-ḥilli* (Poetry collection), dār ṣābir, Beirut.

Al-Bustani, M., *al-tafsīr al-bināʾi li al-Qurʾan al-karīm* (Structural meaning of the Qurʾan), viewed 6 June 2013, <www.alseraj.net/a-k/Qran/al-tafseer/01/fehrsl. htm>.

Al-Durubi, I. 2001, *al-baghdādiyyūn, ʾakhbāruhum wa majālisuhum* (Baghdadis and their gatherings), introduction by ʾUsama al-Naqshabandi, 2nd edn, Ministry of Education, dār al-shuʾun al-thaqāfiyya al-ʿamma, Baghdad.

Al-Haydari, Sh. 2008, ṣafahāt min tārīkh al-kutub wal-kutubiyyin fī suq al-Sarāy (History of books in suq al-Sarāy), *al-Mawrūth Journal*, vol. 7, viewed 6 June 2013, <www.iraqnla.org/fp/journal7/23.htm>.

Al-Janabi, B. 2009, 'tārīkh Baghdad yastarkhī fī ḍilāl maqhā al-Khaffāfīn' (History of Baghdad and the coffee shop of al-Khaffāfīn), viewed 3 June 2013, <www. aljanabi.com>.

Al-Khazraji, N. 2008, 'taqāsīm al-qafza al-ʾadabiyya fī al-ʾalfiyya al-thāniya al-ḥijriyya' (Literature growth in the second *hijri* millennium), *al-ḥiwār al-muta-maddin*, no. 2156, <www.ahewar.org/debat/show.art.asp?aid=121268#>.

Al-Qurʾan, <https://quran.com/>.

Al-Rumaythi, J., 'maqāhi Baghdad' (The coffee shops of Baghdad), viewed 3 June 2013, <https://sites.google.com/site/elkarbalaee/baghdadcoffieshops>.

Al-Saʿdi, M.R. (ed.) 1902, *diwān shaykh Kazim al-ʾUzari al-Baghdadi* (Poetry collection of al-ʾUzari), al-maṭbaʿa al-mustafawiyya, Bombay, <www.Al-mostafa.com>.

Al-Saghir, M.H., 'taṭawwur al-baḥth al-dalālī fī al-Qurʾan al-karīm' (The development of emblematical research of the *Qurʾan*), mawsūʿat al-dirāsāt al-qurʾaniyya, pp. 22–24, viewed 6 June 2013, <www.alseraj.net/maktaba/kotob/quran/tatawer/01. html#2>.

Al-Waʾili, A. 1980, diwān al-Waʾili (Poetry collection of al-Waʾili), 1st edn, ʾahl al-Bayt Press, Beirut, viewed 20 July 2011, <www.al-waʾeli.com>.

Al-Warid, B.A. 1980, *ḥawādith Baghdad fī 12 qarn* (The events of Baghdad in 12 centuries), al-dār al-ʿarabiyya, Baghdad.

Al-Zarkali, Kh. 1978, *al-aʿalām* (The notables), al-Warrak Publishing Ltd, London, viewed 9 June 2013, <www.alwaraq.net/Core/waraq/coverpage?bookid=511&option=1>.

Bayat, M.M. 2008, *Fuduli al-Baghdadi: shaʿir ʾahl al-Bayt* (Fuduli: Poet of the Prophet's household), Bizturkmeniz, <www.bizturkmeniz.com/ar/showArticle.asp?id=13397>.

Jawad, M. & Susa, A. 1958, *Dalil kharitat Baghdad al-Mufassal fī khitat Baghdad qadiman wa-hadithan* (Detailed guide of Baghdad maps), al-Majmaʿ al-ʿIlmi al-Iraqi, Baghdad.

Jawad, M., Susa, A., Makkiya, M. & Maʿruf, N. 1968, *Baghdad*, Iraqi Engineers Association with Gulbenkian Foundation, Baghdad.

Khayyat, J. (ed.) 1968, *ʾarbaʿat qurūn min tārīkh al-Iraq al-ḥadīth* (Four centuries of modern Iraq), by Stephen Hemsley Longrigg, Baghdad.

Khulusi, S. (ed.) 1962, *tārīkh Baghdad: hadiqat al-Zawrāʾ fī sīrat al-wuzarāʾ by ʾabd al-Rahman al-Suwaidi* (History of Baghdad and the biography of its rulers), vol. 1, maṭbaʿat al-Zaʿim, Baghdad.

Lankarani, M. 1949, *madkhal al-tafsīr* (Introduction to Qurʾanic explanation), markaz fiqh al-aʾimma al-aṭhār, p. 205, viewed 6 June 2013, <www.alseraj.net/maktaba/kotob/quran/Tafsir/Tafsir.html>.

Makkiyya, M. (ed.) 2005, *Baghdad*, 1st edn, al-Warrak Publishing Ltd, London.

Maʿruf, N. 2005, 'al-ḥayāt al-thaqāfiyya fī Baghdad' (Educational life in Baghdad), in Makkiyya, M. (ed.), *Baghdad*, 1st edn, al-Warrak publishing Ltd, London.

Muhammad Ali, I.M. 2008, *madīnat Baghdad: al-abʿad al-ʾijtimāʿiyya wa ẓurūf al-nashʾa* (The founding of Baghdad and its social aspects), al-ḥaḍāriyya lil-ṭibaʿa wal-nashr, al-ʿArif lil-maṭbuʿāt, Baghdad.

Naji, H., 'simāt al-ʿaṭa al-fikrī fī al-qarn al-thāmin al-ḥijrī' (Intellectual products of the eighth *hijri* century), in *majmaʿ al-lugha al-ʿarabiyya*, viewed 6 June 2013, <www.majma.org.jo/majma/index.php/2009-02-10-09-36-00/273-63-7.html>.

Oghlu, F.Y. 2011, *Fuduli al-Baghdadi: sulṭān al-shuʾaraʾ al-turkmān* (Fuduli: King of Turkmans poets), Eskitisin, Kirkuk, <http://eskitisin.net/adab/turk%20sairlari/fuduli%2002.html>.

Rauf, I.A. (ed.) 1978, *tārīkh hawādith Baghdad wal-Basra 1186–1192 AH, 1772–1778 AD, by ʾabd al-Rahmān al-Suwaidi* (History of Baghdad and Basra), The Ministry of Education and Arts, Baghdad.

———— 2000, *maʿālim Baghdad fī al-qurūn al-mutaʾkhira* (The features of Baghdad in recent centuries), Bayt al-ḥikma, Baghdad, Iraq.

———— (ed.) 2004, *al-ʿiqd al-lāmiʿ bi-ʾāthār Baghdad wal-masājid wal-jawāmiʿ, by ʾabd al-Hamid Abadah* (Historical mosques of Baghdad), 1st edn, ʾanwār dijl Publishing, Baghdad, p. 20. Also see Jawad, Susa, Makkiyya & Maʿruf, *Baghdad*.

———— (ed.) 2007, *tārīkh al-ʿusar al-ʿilmiyya fī Baghdad, by Muhammad Said al-Rawi al-Baghdadi* (History of knowledgeable families of Baghdad), dār al-shuʾūn al-thaqāfiyya al-ʿamma, al-ʾaʿẓamiyya, Baghdad.

———— (ed.) 2008, ʾakhbār Baghdad wa mā jāwarahā min al-bilād, by Mahmud Shukri al-ʿAlusi (History of Baghdad and its neighbouring countries), al-dār al-Arabiyy a lil-mawsuʿāt, Beirut.

———— 2009, al-tārikh wa al-muʾarrikhūn al-ʿirāqiyyūn fī al-ʿahd al-ʿuthmāni (History and historians during the Ottomans era), al-Warrak Publishing Ltd, Beirut, London.

Selman, A. 2012, 'al-Kazimiyya fī aʿmāq al-tārīkh', *Burāthā News Agency*, viewed 6 June 2013, <www.burathanews.com/news_article_174457.html>.

Selman, I., ʿabd al-Khaleq, H., Al-Izzi, N. & Yunus, N. 1982, al-ʿimarat al-ʿarabiyya al-Islamiyya fī al-Iraq (Arabic and Islamic architecture in Iraq), vols. 1&2, al-Hurriyya Press, Baghdad.

Shubbar, J. 2001, ʾadab al-ṭaff (Karbala literature), vol. 5, muʾassat al-tārīkh, Beirut, viewed 2 June 2013, <http://m-alhassanain.com/kotob%20hossain/adab% 20hosaini/adab%20altaf/index.htm>.

Shukur, Sh. (ed.) 1980, diwān al-ʿUzari al-Kabīr (Poetry collection of al-ʿUzari), dār al-tawjih al-Islami, Beirut.

Susa, A. 1952, *Atlas Baghdad*, mudiriyyat al-masāḥa al-ʿāmma, Baghdad.

———— 1968, 'ray Baghdad, qadiman wa hadithan' (The irrigation of Baghdad), in *Baghdad, Jawad, Susa, Maʿruf & Makkiyya*, Iraqi Engineers Association with Gulbenkian Foundation, Baghdad.

Index

Note: Page numbers in *italic* indicate a figure.

For Product Safety Concerns and Information please contact our
EU representative GPSR@taylorandfrancis.com Taylor & Francis
Verlag GmbH, Kaufingerstraße 24, 80331 München, Germany